Dawn in the Dooryard

Reflections from the Jagged Edge of America

Timothy Cotton

Down East Books

CAMDEN, MAINE

Down East Books

An imprint of Globe Pequot, the trade division of The Rowman & Littlefield
   Publishing Group, Inc.
4501 Forbes Blvd., Ste. 200
Lanham, MD 20706
www.rowman.com
www.downeastbooks.com

Distributed by NATIONAL BOOK NETWORK

ISBN 978-1-68475-002-3 (cloth)
ISBN 978-1-68475-003-0 (electronic)

♾️™ The paper used in this publication meets the minimum requirements of
American National Standard for Information Sciences—Permanence of Paper for
Printed Library Materials, ANSI/NISO Z39.48-1992.

CONTENTS

Contents

Contents

INTRODUCTION

I'VE DETERMINED THAT THIS INTRODUCTION IS THE MOST challenging part of the book to write. The stories that fill this book came to me much more comfortably—easily, really.

I've finally concluded that I am a writer. I explained to a friend that I tried to keep it a secret from myself. I felt that a public admission, or worse, a declaration, might drop a rusty anvil on how easily some stories drift into my mind. Suddenly, my lifelong affliction of excessive daydreaming made more sense to me. Whether the world agrees with me or not, I am—at least—a writer. I could not tell someone that with a straight face for a time. I can say it now.

I always knew I was a cop—and so did everyone else. You don't have to explain to people that you're a police officer; it's implied every day by the uniform, the equipment, the car, and the host of problems that the world asks you to solve.

There is no standardized color or uniform style when you are a writer. While I was proud to wear "the bag" for thirty-four years, I'm relieved that I will never have to don it again. Uniforms become restrictive for a boatload of reasons; to turn them in to the supply officer is the visual and physical statement of a changing life.

My home closet space now appears more significant. The plaid flannels that were once separated by short and long-sleeved dark blue uniform shirts seem now—in the emptiness—remarkably similar in both color and pattern. Creatures of habit rarely heed the lessons that should have been gleaned from forced viewings of "What Not to Wear."

Writers have no dress code, and no one expects them to mitigate often-unsolvable problems. I have found that I can utilize many of the same facial expressions in both careers, so that's a win. I will no longer select my sports jackets for the express reason of allowing better concealment of a firearm. Who knows, maybe I'll become stylish.

My close friends are not writers, and very few of them read my stuff. Occasionally, during periods of jest, they take friendly jabs and make humorously derisive comments about choosing writing as my second career. I often remind them that words are easy; putting them together in the proper order has got me flummoxed. We laugh, but they don't realize that I am not kidding—at all.

The order of the words is so essential—not to please grammarians, and certainly with no bowing to critics. The order of the words must make *me* feel as if I've been successful in sharing my stories with you. I'll never make it to the top of the lists for the lauded, but I will walk away knowing I've been faithful to the stories that float around within my head like maple leaves released from branches by invisible yet mighty autumn winds. Many of those stories have settled on these pages.

As for *Dawn in the Dooryard*, it's a collection of stories because I am a collection of stories, just like you are.

Thanks for picking up my books.
Your friend,
Tim

A Brief History of Utility Trailers

My grandfather's utility trailer was bolted to a heavy-duty set of leaf springs and perched on an old car or truck axle. It was constructed of plywood and painted "porch floor" gray. He did not have a pickup truck because he didn't need one.

I most enjoyed the times that we grandkids were allowed to ride amongst the garbage bags and household refuse for the short ride to the dump. I think he always had the safety chains attached, but things were different in the '70s. Personal safety really was an afterthought, and I don't recall anyone ever mentioning that it wasn't a good idea.

I am reasonably certain Grampa loved us. Mainly because I could see him check for us in the rearview mirror every now and then.

An early adopter of being "green," Gramps did not want his garbage or his grandkids just left in the center of the road. Looking back, I remember the smell was not that of roses, and sitting on the wheel well while grasping the ever-flexing side panels would keep you out of the stinkiest of the garbage.

In a world awash with the smell of old tuna cans, bleach bottles, and the exhaust fumes of a fire engine red, 1970 Plymouth Valiant, life was grand. Watery eyes were welcome as it helped wash the wind-driven coffee grounds and road dust from my prepubescent corneas.

The ubiquitous utility trailer is a part of life in rural New England. While pickup trucks have taken over as the ride of choice, it was not too long ago that the home-built trailer was how you moved the dirty stuff in and out of your life. Sure, curbside garbage pickup was an option in the more suburban parts of Maine, but there were not many suburban parts in Maine. This still holds true. There is some satisfaction in being immersed in the solid waste pipeline to and from your home.

Automobiles of the '70s were equipped with steel bumpers. Your local mechanic could add a trailer hitch, but so could anyone with an adjustable wrench and socket set.

Utility trailers were usually home-built and relatively unsafe. Mismatched bias-ply tires and old studded snow tires shared the same axle and sang different tunes on the asphalt. Trailer sway could be mitigated by adding or subtracting a little speed. Safety chains were crucial, but two of them were not always used. We have come a long way.

The "homemade" utility trailer is becoming a thing of the past. You can go to any big box or building supply store and pick up a properly manufactured utility trailer at a reasonable price. There are trailer-specific outlets as well.

If you don't own a trailer, you will be borrowing from a friend. Here are a few tips to make it go well:

- Request the trailer in person, at least one week in advance. Other people might have dibs for the period that you need the trailer. Most owners know that they cannot use the trailer during Peak Borrowing Season. In New England, P-B-S runs from April 1 through July 4 and then from September 1 through December 15. Basically, this covers spring cleanup and then fall firewood season. Trailer owners have four whole months to use the trailer outside the Peak Borrowing Season. Plenty of time to get their chores done.

- Make sure to notify the owner if you do not have the correctly sized trailer ball. You will, of course, require the owner to supply you with the receiver bar and ball. There is no reason to buy a hitch as long as your vehicle has the receiver. This is what friends are for.

- Ask the trailer owner to ensure that the tires are aired up to the proper psi for the load you will carry. Just another reason why you should notify them at least a week in advance.

- Request that the trailer owner removes all the debris and material from the trailer's bed far in advance of your planned pickup. Do not fall for the "old switcheroo." This is a ploy of many experienced trailer owners. They tend to leave the load of firewood or concrete blocks on their trailer after making a pickup. They then will grant permission to you to borrow the trailer, and pretty soon, you have been drafted into unwanted manual labor. Do not become a victim. Plan to do a drive-by before requesting a trailer. Trailers are kept in backyards and behind garages. Recon will save you backaches and harsh feelings toward a trailer owner that tries to use you for free labor. If the trailer is loaded, find another friend with a trailer.

One great way to keep track of friends with trailers and stay true to your desire to reuse and recycle is to keep all of those family-portrait holiday cards that pile up around Christmas. You know—the glossies that hang on the fridge so that you can remember how many kids your friends have. Usually, those cards include names and ages.

Here is the trick. Use the cards to remind yourself what size utility trailer that particular family owns. Jot the information down on the back of the card and file it appropriately.

A side benefit is to note each of the kids' ages and working abilities depicted on those cards. So, when help is needed to remove a brush pile from your property or load the trailer with anything labor-intensive, you'll know where healthy teens are available for recruitment. After all, this is about you. The kids will feel important when you ask for them by name. You should pay them. It's the polite thing to do.

You can also rent a trailer from many locations. Still, it seems silly to spend good money when you can plan accordingly and borrow one. There are times when trailer owners are selfish and need to use the trailer themselves. Try to be understanding of their plight.

Borrowing is nourishment for the bond of friendship. Just make sure you return it so that the next person who needs it can grab it before Peak Borrowing Season is over.

A Cloaked Visitor Called Autumn

Standard late-August conversations with like-minded individuals are often peppered with the A-word.

There is a distinct odor that permeates Maine air in mid- to late August. I caught a whiff of it late one night. The scent was earthy, not quite musty. It drifts in with very little fanfare.

Certainly, I would be fibbing if I told you that it didn't make me feel a bit older. But it also comes preinstalled with some strange and calming anesthesia, a numbness, really. Maybe that's an overstatement. I've tried—for years—to put the feeling into words. With most of my feelings, my words can't do the feeling justice. Writing about it—for me—somehow makes me believe that I'm able to capture it.

The best I can do is call it a comfortable acceptance; it's autumn, and it's in the air. There is no taking it back.

Those of you in the lower tiers of our great nation will still swelter for a time, and we will, too, on certain days.

For the foreseeable future, evenings will allow glimpses of the cloaked intruder who will slowly change the feel of the air on your face and reveal slight changes in the color of the landscape at every sunrise.

Autumn will be shunned by a few, at least for a time. She will be referred to as a visitor by some. The comfortable acceptance of her paintbrush—and her cool, numbing touch—will soon follow.

Getting older is also more acceptable when accompanied by an old friend called Autumn.

A Mild Rant from 2020

The Internet memes are freshly made and are distributed by Zuckerberg's delivery truck with nary a request from the masses; they keep coming.

It's the day after political debate in America. We have a pandemic on our hands, Harvey Weinstein is hospitalized with a ticker issue, and the stock market took a first-class free dive into the shallow end of the pool that holds my retirement savings plan.

Later, we will be prodded by others sharing these informative memes twenty to thirty times. Then, our friends and coworkers hold up their phones to display their favorite; and they are always willing to send one to you in an email or text message.

Tonight—before bed—we will see the same memes a couple more times as our compadres with slower Internet connections discover all this fodder for the first time, and the sharing begins anew.

It's like finding stale doughnuts that ooze the original cooking oil after you run them through twenty seconds in the Amana radar range, late at night, while everyone else has given up on that last doughnut in the box—but you are not a quitter.

We would all be better served—and happier—if we could eschew the political memes, do some deeper reading on our favorite (and not-so-favorite) candidates, and glean information about all the other important issues while we are at it.

I even see memes about the Coronavirus! Have we no shame?

When I write something that is "too long for the Internet"—meaning more than ten sentences—I research the shares in a quest to see how many people start their commentary with "It's a little long, but it might be worth the read!" I find many.

My stuff is not essential in the scheme of our ongoing quest to navigate through our short time on earth. Sure, it kills some time, but staying informed is very important. Even my written stuff might be considered a long meme, with no photos.

I just hope you don't base your opinions, future investments, children's well-being, decisions on whom you will spend your life with, or dietary choices on the memes that some twenty-nine-year-old created after snipping screenshots from the television. I picture them in my mind, posting while they wait for the Hot Pocket to cool down enough to eat without taking the skin off the top of their mouth.

My suggestion—and maybe I should have made this a meme—is to go to a library, a bookstore, a newspaper stand (are there any left?). Heck, watch a couple of decent documentaries.

Read something that *is* a little long—maybe even force yourself to turn some actual numbered paper pages!

A Nice Guy

I wasn't trying to be nosy, but I cannot deny that I listened to the conversation between the store employee and the patron who waited his turn at getting to the cream dispenser.

It was a counter area where I don't spend much time, and I will grudgingly admit that there are a few days each year when I add one sugar and one cream to my coffee.

There is no rhyme or reason to when that happens, but it does. I take it black on all the other days.

I was on one of my jaunts to nowhere in particular, and it struck me that a little bit of sugar might aid me in ridding myself of a slight headache. I'd been driving for about an hour and a half, with about thirty minutes left to my final destination. There are times in life when you want something sweet.

The store employee was methodically refilling the refrigerated countertop cream and milk dispenser while the two of us waited her out. The man in front of me knew the lady, and they talked about the sudden loss of a mutual friend. We will call him Jerry.

"That was awful quick, and he was such a nice guy," she said.

"Cancer, no one even knew until he was in bed permanently. He was a tough bird."

The man had a distinct Maine accent. It was thick, with a bit of a whine. Some say that a true Maine accent sounds a bit like "crying between the words." Maybe that "someone" is me, but I heard it somewhere else first. Some friends from the west coast claim that I have a slight accent. I disagree.

My compadre of the coffee condiment counter had his hair styled the same way my dad and my uncles presented their hair in the early '70s. It was neat, with just the right amount of product; combed over, with a distinct part on the right side. I would describe it as a more modernized version of the D/A style. Some—here—will know what I mean.

He had the weathered appearance of a man who spent some time outside, on the coast. His jeans were dark blue, unfaded with orange stitching, and they were neatly pressed. I surmised that he wasn't working today.

The back of his plaid shirt was bloused—and tucked in—properly. You don't see that much. He had been in the military a long time ago, or he was raised by a man who was.

He told the milk lady that he was heading to town to get his COVID shot. It suddenly made sense to me. He came up in an era when you dappered-up a bit to go to an appointment.

I was raised the same way. For some reason, I dropped that charade a long time ago. I think it's a rebellious message meant to push back against the grain of a life spent inside uniforms with polished shoes and black polyester clip-on ties. I still have my court suits. They are slowly going out of style, fading further back into the recesses of the closet. I don't tuck on days off. I feel okay about it.

I envied his commitment to looking sharp for a needle stick that might make his life easier. I'd been inoculated for months. It had all but slipped my mind that many of Maine's rural folks were longing to be vaccinated. Most would have given their right arm for the special treatment I had received while getting my shots—earlier—due to my current occupation. I am by no means special, but the job put me near the top of the list for first dibs on shots. The government made the list; I just complied.

I could tell he was pleased that he had secured an appointment. I can't say why I knew it, but I did. Inflection means far more than the words that are shared. I was happy for him; it would probably take a load off his mind. He was just about my age, right in the sweet spot of folks who could be more debilitated by the onset of the strange virus.

I looked at his right hand. It held one paper cup filled with hot black coffee. In his meaty left paw, he held an empty paper cup.

It confused me at first, but he explained it to me like we were old friends. He didn't just blurt out the reason. I had asked, under my breath, where the coffee stirrers were. He pointed them out. I saw the individually wrapped, thin plastic straws in a bin right in front of my face.

"You need four of 'em to stir a cup of coffee, so I do what I used to do when I was drinking." He held up the two cups and mimicked the pouring of one into the other.

Several of his fingernails appeared to have been slammed—hard—into some painful mechanical contraptions. They clearly had been utilized to pry him out of some difficult situations. He was a tradesman of some type, possibly a fisherman enjoying a rare day off.

"Once I put the cream in, I mix it by pouring them back and forth between the cups. Wastes a paper cup, but it saves on plastic stirrers. Damn things are so small that they don't even move the coffee around in the cup."

"It makes sense," I said. And it did. It made perfect sense.

We watched the clerk manipulating the machine so that it would soon supply the cow-created creamy goodness to the parade of coffee drinkers who would march by over the next three hours.

In that short moment in time, I found out that Jerry had passed away from cancer and that the man in the plaid shirt was a recovering drinker who was kind and considerate to share his method of perfectly mixing a cup of coffee with cream and sugar. He didn't have to do that, but he did. That might not be a big deal to you when you are in a hurry, but it made me feel accepted in an unfamiliar environment.

We waited as the lady attendant made sure that the clear plastic bag filled with half & half was metering correctly out of the cream dispenser.

I grabbed a single packet of sugar and dumped it into my cup of coffee. I used two of the plastic straws to stir it rapidly. The man was right; the damn things barely moved the coffee around in the cup. His hypothesis had, now, become a proven theory. I skipped the cream out of respect for the kind man's process. He didn't need me hanging around behind him—waiting—while he mixed up his coffee.

I walked to the register as I reflected on how fast Jerry had been taken from them. In that short memorial service for a nice guy, I had learned a lot. I wondered how Jerry liked his coffee.

The clerk offered me a reasonably priced club membership for future discounts on coffee; I declined. I told her that I didn't live in the area, so it wouldn't do me much good. Of course, she already knew it.

I nodded my head back toward the man who had unknowingly made the stop worthwhile.

"I want to take care of his coffee too." The clerk punched in the extra and I paid the bill. He raised his single cup toward me in a toast and said, "Hey, thanks!"

I could see that he now held a quart of motor oil in his other hand, probably destined for the truck with the opened hood parked out by the gas pumps. I wish I had seen the 5w30 as it would have been the gracious thing to pay for it. We could have talked about how many miles were on the Ford. It would have been pleasant to find some confirmation for my hasty conclusions. None of it was any of my business, so I determined to just move along and try to nurse away my headache with some improperly mixed Rwandan roast with one sugar.

As I pushed the door open, I heard him say to the clerk, "He was a nice guy. Do you know him?" The door shut behind me, cutting off the conversation, but I know she told him that she didn't.

It's good that Jerry had a lasting impact on his friends. I surmised that he'd be happy that they remembered him as being worthy of a mention during an important moment in the everyday life. I was pleased enough to have entered the ebb and flow of the imaginary club for nice guys.

I didn't buy his coffee to be considered with that kind of reverence, of course. I bought it to show a tiny bit of bean-infused gratitude for small favors, and maybe because, in a world filled with people who sometimes cause me frustration, he made me feel at ease for fifteen seconds. That's worth a buck seventy-nine all day long.

I pulled the shifter into drive and waited for a few miles to take the first sip. There are times in life when you want something sweet.

A PRECARIOUS PILE

THE PRECARIOUS PILE OF PERSONAL ITEMS THAT HAVE PRO-
truded upward—to a pinnacle—will soon require "perusement"—it's a word—and subsequent replacement.

*(Editor's note—"Perusement" is not a word, but you try dealing
with him. Tim's explanation is "It should be; therefore, it is.")*

The Red Wings were a last-minute addition to the pile
when I realized that Ronnie the Roomba was hungry for boot
laces. One of the poor fellows was dragged all the way to the
dining room. It was the right boot, and it was not lost on me
that it could somehow represent our current societal situation.

I put them back together in hopes of reconciliation. I need
them both to continue walking forward. Shoes should not be
dragged into the political arena or over to the dining room table.

Ronnie has no patience for fools who leave their shoes
around; I'll do better.

My significant One has limited my counter and table space,
and rightly so. I have been relegated to improvising. I cannot
say that I am adapting very well to a lack of a flat area that is
suitable for piling.

The dump-recovered Klipsch speakers are sturdy enough to
hold their own. Or, in this case, my own while they pump out
mood-edited genres of confusing music mixes.

Sinatra, AC/DC, Ray LaMontagne, Van Hagar, and Old
Dominion spend afternoons together. At the same time, they

are blasted forth by the moldy music makers, pumped up in power by a small Amazon-supplied Bluetooth amplifier. The amplifier is also covered by a pile of receipts and a soft cleaning cloth for my eyeglasses.

By fifty-seven, a man knows his strengths and his weaknesses. It used to be that I believed that more storage containers were the answer. That was a failure of the first order.

Storage containers do not allow you to see your things. I am visual. If I can't see it, at least at some point, I will forget all about it. The benefit is that when I do find it, I am overwhelmed with the discovery, pleased that I have it, and I place it out in the open so that I never lose it again.

My storage containers become empty, and I tend to pile them up—unencumbered by freight—in the basement corner that I rarely utilize.

I cannot say that I have given up because I am continuously trying to figure out the best way to be organized. I will admit that I am not willing to completely reinvent myself.

That pile will surely be sturdy enough to hold up a couple more books. The boots will be removed today. I need them for walking.

A Stump for Standing

When the broken hemlock was removed—and it was a big one—my woods neighbor utilized cable and hydraulics to winch it out of there.

He sawed the remainder off but left the big stump a little high. He told me that he thought I might use it as a table or a seat for sitting and thinking.

That's the thing about a good stump.

There are mornings I stand on the stump and take a few sips of coffee while the dog goes about sniffing and snorting up the news.

No one sees me standing on the stump, so I don't dress up to do it. I'll say no more than that.

When the fog subsides, it's an excellent spot to watch the world stand still as you do the same.

Years ago, I went to speak at a small college in Appalachia that has a beautiful museum dedicated to Abraham Lincoln. I might be incorrect, but I believe that Lincoln Memorial University in Harrogate, Tennessee, has the most extensive collection of Lincoln memorabilia and artifacts anywhere in the world. I was starstruck on my tour. "Starstruck" is such a stupid word, but it described my feelings quite well.

I was even allowed into the special vault where I could hold in my hand cuttings of the hair from Abraham, Mary Todd, and Willie Lincoln. Of course, the curator supplied special gloves and gave me clear directions and warnings about the proper way to handle the packaged locks in my open palm. That was surreal.

I was also able to scroll through the pages of a book that had an actual handwritten signature from every United States president up to that point. That was a kick, and being a huge fan of Teddy Roosevelt, I studied his signature for a very long time.

Odd, museum curators don't ever seem to be in a big rush. There is a good chance that overseeing history makes them very patient humans.

I digress.

I stood on the stump for a while this morning, and it reminded me of one of my favorite quotes from Lincoln. Of course, he was making a political speech. I was just standing there, pleased that no one was looking at all. I sense—from his writings—that Abe Lincoln was a big fan of self-deprecation. I respect that.

I have stepped out upon this platform that I may see you and that you may see me, and in the arrangement, I have the best of the bargain.—Abraham Lincoln, 1861

The fog bank lifted off to reveal another fantastic day on the jagged edge of America.

A Western Drive with Sinatra

Sinatra accompanied me home last night. My guilty pleasure is not cable television. Oh, I have cable, and I bounce between a total of four channels. But it's radio—delivered by a satellite hanging in low orbit—that brings me the most joy for my entertainment dollar.

I usually leave eastern Washington County, Maine, around mid-afternoon. For various reasons—some good—I went during the late-summer sunset.

A low ceiling of clouds made the sunset appear as a mere sliver of elongated orange fire. I felt like a boy watching a ballgame through a crack in the right-field fence.

I don't have a Stetson; I don't even wear hats very often. I merely imagined that view from under a Stetson. I've probably watched too much *Yellowstone*. I listened to the Sinatra channel playing "Summer Wind" for what must be the fiftieth time in the last several months.

Sure, it was recorded live. Last night's version was recorded in Paris, I think.

Visions of being a cowboy don't compute with mid-century crooning; it doesn't have to. It's my vision, and I'll listen to whatever I want while I contemplate a trip west in a modern-day gas-fed Conestoga.

The recently plucked blueberry fields that pepper Washington County give you quick glimpses of a prairie-like drive. Gnarled spruce, hemlock, and pine will intervene shortly, and the distant and uncatchable sunset disappears as it's drawn into the crooked tips of branches that reliably steal the show as if you've been kicked out of your own imagination.

Cutting it close to the shoreline—and the mighty Atlantic—as Route 1 tends to do, I searched for some Carolina Shag. I guess the channel has been suspended for a time. It's too bad because I really enjoyed it a couple of years ago as I drove through North Carolina in the dark.

I tried to listen to some comedy, but it seems that some comics have concluded that F-bombing my dark drive home is the only way to make me laugh. Three minutes of that was enough, and I found some Fogelberg on The Bridge.

There was a time when I would have laughed more at that stuff, but I've heard it—too many times—from pissed-off people who really should work on their repertoire of anger-driven diatribes.

Plus, Ellie, the Lab-boxer mix, was in the back looking out her own window; she's only five and doesn't need to pick up another bad habit. The begging for snacks is annoying enough. If she starts F-bombing me while I finish my French fries, I guess I'll just turn up the Sinatra.

AIR CONDITIONING IS ONLY ONE AVAILABLE OPTION

THE LATE-AFTERNOON HEAT CAUSED ME TO GRIPE—internally—about my early-morning choice of mechanical conveyance.

My discount capsule of transportation—also known as the green glider—was chosen because I had accepted the weatherman's promise of slightly less humidity.

The green glider's air-conditioning button does glow green when depressed, but that, right there, is where the dream of dry armpits ends.

The air-conditioning system needs to be recharged, but I believe it needs much more than that. I am not going to spend any money fixing it up; it's my winter car, currently being utilized as my summer car.

It's confusing to some, but not to me. It provides me about double the distance on a gallon of gas than my pickup truck. It smells like the ghost of a wet golden retriever, and the fan belt squeals upon start-up. The stereo works quite well, and three of the four electric windows work with reasonable reliability.

I left the windows open a crack for the entire day. I believe that it vents out at least some of the heat that is deposited within as it sits in the relentless sun.

Upon start-up, I roll 'em all down, and I make my way along Main Street to catch an on-ramp to I-395 for the drive home. Tonight, while stopped at each of the four dreaded red lights, I realized I was the only person driving with my windows down.

I don't feel the need to socialize at stoplights, not at all. But I think we are missing out on some of the simple pleasures that sweltering stops used to bring us back in the days before air conditioning was a standard amenity.

What I am missing are the commonalities that can be gleaned from sitting still—for a moment—and listening to music coming from the car in the next lane over.

I miss hearing late-afternoon AM radio newscasts delivered by deep-voiced men and sultry-sounding ladies. I miss Looking Glass providing the one-millionth playing of "Brandy" and then quickly searching my analog radio dial for the same station so I can hear it, firsthand, from my own dilapidated speakers.

I long to hear the tapping of wedding bands on the smooth steering wheels when a song takes the driver's attention away from what could have been a very bad day. I miss the whiff of cigarette smoke from tired and sweaty tradesmen wearing dirty white T-shirts while they are headed home from the grind. They sit still, lustfully longing for three cold Buds along with homemade meatloaf and two baked potatoes.

Maybe they would have a chance to play catch in the street for ten minutes after the dishes were done. Ultimately, they would probably fall asleep in their chair before the newscasters toss it over to the weather prognosticator.

Sure, we were all in our own little world; each of us an anonymous understudy to actors who were playing in nearby theaters. We were a gaggle of vinyl-benched bit players in bands heading to different towns.

We used to be alone, but we were still together; it doesn't feel that way anymore.

I miss the simple novellas that were hastily written about our lives as we unintentionally intersected at city stoplights. Roll down your windows; air conditioning isn't all that it's cracked up to be.

AJA

I WENT TO BED WITH INTENTIONS OF READING FOR A VERY long time; that's why I started early.

That didn't work out, and I suppose—for Ellie's sake—it was a cruel joke to disappear into the sheets and comforter without a final salutation. Sure, she kissed me goodnight; she always does.

I had adjusted her collar because of our shared dilemma of winter-like weight being added during our summer season. I told her that I hadn't had to adjust my belt yet, but I did sense a bit of discomfort that I hoped might force me to walk by all pasta dishes because of a lingering sense of constriction.

She wandered away when she noted that the book was drawing more of my attention than the incessant pushing of her nose into my left arm. I don't believe I lasted through three pages of Teddy Roosevelt's early years before the book tumbled, and I slipped off into the abyss that called me away from being better informed about iconic presidents.

I share all this only to relay that 0200 hours came at me like the ringside bell at the end of a prizefight in a musty gym. I opened my eyes to wonder where I was for a moment. A glance at the dark figure on my far right cleared out the cobwebs.

Ellie's silhouette is unique, sort of like Batman—but only if the ears on his mask had not been docked and made into sharp points. She made no noise, but her eyes must send out waking beams similar to those of Titano, the DC Comic-derived "super ape."

Titano's eyes sent forth a kryptonite beam, but I don't think that Ellie's do. Her's are merely vibes of negativity from being disgusted at the length of time since the last potty break.

She made not a peep. It's creepy to be stared at. Cute, but weird. I got up.

After some eye rubbing and coffee, we made our way to the outer perimeter wood line at Chez Timmaay. Upon our return, I somehow fell into the abyss provided by a film documenting the making of Steely Dan's *AJA* album.

Knowing very little about jazz/rock/blues fusion music, the 1977 production from Fagen and Becker mesmerized me when I was fourteen. So much so that I burned through two cassettes and one CD (later) in my life. Now it's digitized somewhere in my Apple music library.

The documentary was a pleasant way to prepare for a day of rain coming toward us.

The YouTubes do provide some really great things at terrible times. On mornings like this, I don't curse the Interweb the same way that I condemn the offerings from cable television. I am pleased to embrace old documentaries, even if just to avoid the overly intimate toy commercials and the AM Gold offerings from Time/Life music. Frankly, the documentary is fantastic.

Tonight, I will try to avoid reading in bed. But I think Teddy would have enjoyed "Deacon Blues."

I digress.

Angel in the Rain

Her summer dress was the color of autumn, and it followed her slight figure effortlessly down the sidewalk. Her pin-straight posture drew my attention, but not for the reason one might assume.

The July downpour was violent, and I had just driven through the worst of it at a rate far slower than commonly carries me to my destinations. My wipers wanted to do more for me, but they begged for my forgiveness with each futile swipe.

I saw her from a distance; she was alone and moving with purpose. What surprised me was that she lacked the urgency that one would expect from a human who was caught in a storm, unaware.

As I closed the distance, I noted that her hands were stretched forward slightly. Her palms were directed—upward—toward the sky. The smile on her face might have concerned someone who did not recognize the difference between pure joy and the onset of madness. She was not mad.

I would describe her pose, her positioning, as that of an angel who was beckoning an earthly being to remain calm in the face of an unexpected celestial apparition.

Even now, my description sounds like I might have been confronted by madness, but there she was, smiling.

She was smiling about being caught in the rain. Her joy was evident, and it was appreciated. For a short time, as I passed, I was jealous that I, too, had not been caught in the rain.

Her summer dress was the color of autumn, and it followed her slight figure effortlessly down the sidewalk. Her pin-straight posture drew my attention, but not for the reason you had assumed.

26

BLACK COFFEE, A NICE BREEZE, AND MY FAVORITE JEANS

I SIPPED A BLACK COFFEE AND LEANED AGAINST THE OPEN tailgate of the truck. I noted a sheen of the spilled bar and chain oil and made a concerted effort to keep my favorite jeans from brushing against the residual result of my rush to fill the old chainsaw earlier today.

The caffeine-infused epiphany that my best pair of jeans already had some slightly faded oil stains on the area just above the knee enticed me to hop up onto the tailgate. This was in total defiance of the high probability that my buttocks would soon carry similar stains, regardless of my caution or care.

I closed my eyes to feel more of the breeze. In the same way that people turn down the radio to locate an address or a difficult-to-pinpoint driveway, closing my peepers helped me focus on the pleasant few minutes before I resumed the drive home.

I discovered, just this year, that I tend to close my eyes when I brush my teeth. Not all the time, of course. It's my way of stealing back just a little more rest from the night before. I guess I close them now and then when I brush my teeth before bed too. I think during those times that I am just practicing for what I hope is soon to come.

There is rarely an attractive moment to be glimpsed when I'm brushing my teeth. Maybe you are different. We all have positive attributes, but some are given less than others. I've accepted my deficit. Tooth brushing should not be a time when we worry about whether we're an appealing specimen.

I admit that I sometimes take a moment to peek at what is in the mirror. I usually close my eyes quickly while embarking on a few seconds of silent prayer. Honestly, I'm hopeful that the man in the mirror will leave and go get a cup of coffee before I must face him again.

I digress.

When the breeze diminished, I reopened my eyes to a view of the gas pumps. My hair used to move a bit more than it does now when the wind blows. Was the wind stronger when I was younger? Probably not. I think I may just be giving the wind less to work with.

I sipped the coffee again; the liquid had reached the all-important temperature that allows for longer sips. Longer sips allow more fleeting thoughts. More fleeting thoughts turned to the consideration that I had probably sat far too long in the residual bar and chain oil. The good news was that I was still wearing my favorite jeans, and I needed to finish the remainder of my drive.

I threw an old bath towel over the driver's seat, attempting to protect it from the transfer of oil stains from my favorite jeans to the truck's upholstery. I turned the key to the "on" position, and I was immediately comforted by the fact that Boz Scaggs hadn't turned over the spotlight to Steve Lukather's guitar solo—not yet anyway.

"Breakdown" includes one of the best intros for a radio DJ to verbally assault you with a quick rundown of the time and temperature. I tried to avoid it back in the day. The opening guitar, drum, and keyboard work should be heard and not destroyed by the voice of the ever-present vocalized ego of the radio guy.

I was pretty sure that my previous position on the tailgate had added some oily character to my favorite jeans, but it was worth the time and effort to sit—well-lubricated—on the tailgate for a few minutes. I contemplated whether or not there was a bottle of Dawn dish detergent under the sink at home. If I hustled, I'd be there before the stain had time to set.

Thankfully, I was back at speed by the time Lukather let loose. The quick break from my drive was just what the doctor ordered. I'd be able to keep my eyes wide open for the last sixty-two miles. Good music, a nice breeze, black coffee, and my favorite jeans; I began to wonder how I got so lucky.

Bottoms Up

As I continued my early morning supine supervision of the spinning bedroom ceiling fan while slightly slumbering, I listened intently for the sound of a State Department of Transportation truck slinging snow into driveways as it drove south to north.

Nothing.

I paid scant attention to the details of the forecast last night. I knew that snow would come this morning, but the forecaster wasn't specific on the arrival time. Working to fill Ellie's water dish without turning on the kitchen light was a mistake worthy of TikTok.

I don't use TikTok, but I think placing the side-handled Yeti under the spout of the Keurig—bottom side up—would have only been better if accentuated while being filmed with some tuba music in the background.

The sound of rushing tap water cascading into a stainless-steel dog dish overpowered the metered tinkle of dark-roast coffee rejected by the bottom of a Yeti. That might sound like a wildlife proctologist's nightmare, but it was only mine.

Whoever designed our latest electronic brewing device knew this day would come. The overflow tray beneath the mug captured all but a few splotches of the hot coffee. The blue hand towel that I eschew in favor of a cage-free roll of Bounty cleared the rest from the counter. I flicked on the light over the sink, reloaded the chamber with another cartridge, and made good on the second try.

I wiled away the morning on some writing, watching out the window for the first sign of the storm, waiting for the post office to open, and squinting hard with my left eye while trying to determine if I should have taken the eye doctor up on the progressive lenses. You know, for close work.

The doctor had offered, but I felt that taking off the regular glasses and then squinting would make me appear more thoughtful.

Early rising seems like a good idea on a day off, but you still have to hang around waiting for your destinations to open. Snow had just started falling when I slid the key into the slot on my mailbox. I rummaged through the contents and determined that people should stop sending me mail. The water bill was the only urgent correspondence. The rest of the envelopes found themselves in the recycle bin.

Since I was too early to go to the counter to pick up a package, I left to grab some cash at the bank, but the drive-up window wasn't open yet, either. I drove around the building to access the ATM and then headed back to the post office to finish what I had started.

My trip to the warehouse club found me leaving with a four-pack of low magnification readers, fresh-baked Perdue chicken quarters, red potatoes, and more broccoli than I will be able to ingest in two lifetimes.

Ellie helped me finish a chicken leg for breakfast, and we motored off to the dump, now more appropriately called a transfer station. I still tell the dog we are heading to "the dump," and she never corrects me. She's an old soul, and I appreciate being able to say anything I want without a protest from a passenger.

Now the snow falls heavy on my little burgh. Wind out of the north makes its descent more of a horizontal affair. I made another cup of coffee in my new mug from Swans Island Charters. This time I made sure that it was in the cavern-up position.

The mug is a gift from my brother-in-law. And while he is much too frugal to put his business insignia on an actual Yeti, I can't say that I blame him—they are hard to catch and even harder to hold down for a tattoo.

It's keeping my coffee warm, and it sits nicely on the porch railing while I shovel it off for the second time today. Tonight, when this storm passes, I'll fill up the mug again when I plow up this mess and prepare for what promises to be a beautiful Saturday on the jagged edge of America.

Buy One, Get One

Coffee cooling to an almost acceptable level of tepidity allows multiple scant sips as the gravel turns to macadam and tree-lined roads begin to show signs of increased inhabitation; returning to the workaday world is not really the best way to end any weekend.

The rolling concert that included the Chi-Lites, Spinners, and Aretha was manually interrupted from time to time by Train, The Doobie Brothers, and Van Hagar. During quick stops on the country stations, we pause for a moment or two. But it appears that Luke Bryan is holding a BOGO sale as he dominates the song selection; I don't dislike Luke Bryan, but sometimes I think the station managers threw out all the milk crates full of Merle, Waylon, Johnny Cash, and Charlie Pride albums.

The fresh wax job sheds the mist that is an inevitable airborne side dish, dining and dashing around Down East Maine. It seems fog is the new sunshine—and I love every minute of it.

As a kid banging around the tiny town of Machias, Maine, I recall wearing my daily uniform of an old blue sweatshirt and momma-patched Toughskin pants (trademark and shout-out to Sears and Roebuck). Double knees were a feature of every pair, and I was able to wear a hole in most.

The sweatshirt was a necessity until about 10:30, when the sun would burn through the fog bank that regularly settled down on the little burgh every night. Air-conditioning wasn't necessary, as the Atlantic Ocean provides just the perfect amount of temperature modulation—she is a dependable HVAC technician.

I digress.

Ellie stayed in the back, only barking like a madwoman when a young lady walked too close to the truck during the mandatory fill-up of gasoline near Columbia Falls. I apologized from my position as the hose-man and roadie for the band. The girl was startled, yet sweet, to say, "It's okay. My dog barks when people get close to my car, too." I told her that it was more likely than not that Ellie was attempting to get one of her Doritos and not planning on using force unless she had to. She giggled with a side dish of understanding as she sauntered back to her Malibu—the car, not the famous beach town.

And so, I add an exclamation point to the end of another three-day sentence while incarcerated at a location where I have been overseeing all outside work details for the last twenty-six years. Rocks were removed from the bumpy road, rodents were ridiculed for remaining where they are not welcome, and loons were listened to for clarification on their location and direction of travel.

It's a place where sleep comes easy and driving away comes hard, always tainted with a faint bit of worry that it could be the last trip out. There are no guarantees that the warden doesn't have other plans for this wonderful sentence that we refer to as life.

Cast Iron Stories

Poor planning reared its ugly head at 0337 hours. My nose indicated that I should have put in a little firewood.

I slept with the sliding glass doors wide open, and I was under the impression that the sleeping bag was going to be plenty. Then, dawn showed up and immediately made it clear that her toes were cold.

Ellie began using her nose to nudge me from my slightly chilled slumber. It was a 4:00 o'clock conundrum.

I decided if she was going out, I might as well head to the woodpile to grab a few sticks of yellow birch. This was a summer with very few fires in the wood stove. Usually rainy days—and some Mondays—call for a "smudge" of a fire to dry out your bones. This summer has been very warm with few rain showers.

I found a couple of paper plates that had been thrown in the stove from happier and more festive summer gatherings. I added a few pieces of kindling and discovered that the dormant Vermont Castings stove was still willing to creak and groan to life. Cast iron talks, and it's nice to listen to the stories.

We are cutting wood later today, so this warm little space, complete with a now-snoring dog, is a good reminder of why we cut and split wood in the first place.

We do it because dawn will have cold toes for the foreseeable future. We want to make sure we try to keep her happy.

CEDAR SONGS

IT'S NOT AN ATTRACTIVE TREE, THE CEDAR. I DON'T FIND THEM particularly handsome, but this one is growing extremely close to my dining room window. So close that when the wind comes out of the north—and it does most of the time—it claws at the siding and sometimes bumps the window as if it's demanding permission to enter. I'll trim it when the warmer weather takes up a semipermanent residence at the forty-fifth parallel.

I've given the old cedar very little thought and even less care than I should have. The last time I recall it being trimmed with any purpose was when two-thirds of my family spent an afternoon clipping—and giggling—while perched on a ten-foot aluminum ladder. It was 2010, I am almost sure, and I pulled into the driveway after being on a call-out through the early morning hours. My son and his mom were laughing and holding a now-cordless corded hedge trimmer.

While they both were laughing, my son was sheepishly holding up a freshly cut, orange extension cord that had been recently connected to the power outlet just inside the slightly opened dining room window.

His mother looked at me and asked if I was tired. I nodded but remained focused on the cord situation. Heavy-duty, orange extension cords are expensive. I could tell by the size of the knotted coil on the ground that the frayed end that he was now waving about formerly belonged to my favorite one-hundred-footer. It's a cord that I had used for all kinds of outdoor pursuits that require the delivery of electrons to distant projects.

He piped in, "Well, I already cut off the shorter cord, and this was the only one left." They both started laughing again, and I had no choice but to join in. My laughter was more of a tired acquiescence. Maybe it was a nod to the absurdity of doing the same thing twice and realizing that mistakes are funny when no one has been successfully electrocuted in the process.

We all need to laugh more.

Naturally, his fourteen-year-old, dad-given sarcasm added, "We really should have a gas-trimmer anyway; this thing is junk." I pointed out that it was a Craftsman. It was as if calling out the brand name held some extraordinary power in a day and age when no one else recalled that the word—Craftsman—used to carry a lot of weight for a value-minded shopper.

I am sure that I must have said something about the fact that he could buy a gas trimmer whenever he liked, because that's what dads do. They constantly threaten to make you buy the next one when you act like it doesn't really matter.

The trimming team reverted to long-handled lopping shears at that point. The cedar was younger then, much more supple and pliable. It's gotten older, more gnarled and not so easily trimmed. I have, too.

While that's too much background on my cedar tree, I wanted to introduce you to its forgotten importance in my life. It recently reintroduced itself, but in a most pleasant way. The cedar began to sing.

Just about the time that spring called and mentioned that she might be stopping by, I was almost sure that I heard cardinals singing inside the living room.

It was well after darkness had fallen. My significant other—home for a short window between jobs—was sitting nearby. I asked her if she heard the birds singing. She told me that it must have been the television. The television was powered-up, but the volume was low. The cable receiver was tuned in to The Weather Channel. I surmised that it must have been a sound intertwined within a commercial that I missed.

Two nights later, I heard it again. This time, Ellie was snoozing on the couch beside me. She picked up her head and looked at me as if I was responsible for the song, and then she began to growl. Growling is her go-to vocalization when there is any indication that something is amiss. I shushed her and listened more intently. The clarity of the cardinal song—her last of that night—came from the window in the dining room that overlooks the unkempt cedar.

When I am alone, I dwell in a darkened house. One lamp—sometimes two—illuminates the living room with a warm glow that makes me feel comfortable. I snuck over to the window where my untrimmed cedar stands guard, and I slowly pulled back the curtain. The dusky shadows gave me no insight into the darker-green growth's interior. It was clear that the singer had sensed my presence long before I began to gander through the glass; she was gone.

The following morning—just a few minutes before sun-rise—her tones filled the living room with three or four bursts of calming chords. I had noted the night before that the window latch wasn't firmly locked, and that had some effect on how clearly her songs intruded into my otherwise silent space. It also gave me clarity as to where the draft had been coming from when I walked into the dining area. It was far too late to remedy that for the winter. Still, it was frigidly fortuitous for the spring songs of the lovely lady who found the gnarled cedar to her liking.

She's been back a couple of times. I caught sight of her long tail feathers on a Saturday morning. That was just before she caught sight of the disturbing crow's feet surrounding the blue eyes that searched for her from behind the edge of a curtain. I called my significant other a few minutes later to let her know that I had solved the mystery of the bird songs in the living room. I told her that it wasn't the Weather Channel after all.

That's when we reminisced about the day when she and my son cut two power cords and ended up trimming the—then—songless cedar with shears. We laughed again from a much longer distance than a ten-foot aluminum stepladder could ever span. We determined that was the last time the cedar had been trimmed. I'll have to do it again when warmer weather convenes with more authority.

I still have the Craftsman trimmer. The one-hundred-foot, orange electrical cord has evolved into a less cumbersome ninety-footer.

The reality is that I can probably trim the old cedar by throwing up the sash and reaching out through the window with the old lopping shears. I'll use due caution; I want to make sure that the cardinal feels comfortable when she comes back to sing again.

Chalk

She doesn't know that I watch for her. She pays no mind to my nondescript car passing by her home at just about the same time each morning. The woman is busy; the woman is focused; the woman does not even know who I am. But still, I look forward to seeing her every day.

I've never seen her texting; I have never even seen her with a phone in her hand. She might not have a phone. I don't know. I have never spoken to her; I don't know her name. But I watch for her.

There are days when she looks disheveled, and there are days when she is dressed to the nines—she pays no attention to me—she doesn't even know I'm driving by. She is far too busy to pay attention to the cars that pass.

Some days she wears a ball cap, some days she wears a hoodie, and through the early fall she wore no hat at all. She is focused.

A few weeks ago, I noted that she was drawing on the driveway with a fat piece of chalk. One day it was a cat, and on another day a bunny. I could tell it was a bunny because she was drawing the extra tall ears while down on her hands and knees.

The little boy watches attentively. I don't know if he requests specific chalk-drawn characters or if she might surprise him with her favorites.

Some days she kisses him on the forehead. Probably she does that most days, but I have only witnessed it three or four times. He looks happy, and I am happy for him. His mother is an attentive and loving parent—a parent with chalk. She is an artist. She is a bus stop confidant. She is his mother.

Some days she is listening; some mornings she is talking. He looks at her with an adoring stare. He watches her draw bunnies and cats. He learns from her. I think he is a lucky little boy. And she loves him. I can tell.

The story that unfolds on the side of the road each morning is not the only story, but it is the story that I watch for. I think she is doing a fantastic job raising her son. She loves him, and he loves her. That's all I need to know.

I will never know them; I don't need to. I know enough. Because I watch for them.

Keep your hands to yourself, leave other people's things alone, and be kind to one another.

This piece was written on a whim after weeks of driving by a young lad and his mother as they waited for the school bus. I drove by about the same time each weekday. I wrote it on a yellow sheet of scrap paper on my desk, believing that I could do more with it when I had a chance.

One day, I decided to run it on the BPD Facebook page as it was. I called it "Chalk." While thousands of folks embraced it as an old cop watching out for people—a few found it to be more sinister, as if I were intruding by observing their daily roadside interaction.

The good news is that mom contacted me after her family had read the essay on Facebook. She was delighted by it. She said it made her feel safe and watched over. I later met both the mom and young boy. He made me cookies. The drawing, that I believed was a rabbit, was a huge robot. But my observations about the rest of what I saw were confirmed.

I told her that with all that I have seen in my job, I found the scenes, with her son each day, to be a bit uplifting. I was glad I had written it, and so was she.

The thing is, I understood the concerns that a few people shared. I've been a cop a long time. Working on many crimes against persons, the majority with children as victims, I have lived a life filled with suspicion and questions about motives.

I guess I saw these scenes as parenting as we all should be doing it and I enjoyed observing it from afar. If I had never met them, I still would have believed what I saw was the personification of the true and wholesome love that only a mother can deliver. I'm still glad she called, and that I met them. The cookies were delicious.

Clinging to Almost

There are some days in this career when you think you have all but wasted your time adding touches of gray to the thinning crop on the top of your head. You feel somewhat inadequate at what you have accomplished.

The cases become a blur. You laugh—to yourself—when they tell you that prosecutors dropped another one of your successful investigations, and you begin to tell stories to the younger officers that at one point in your life, you cared just as much as they do now. Of course, they don't believe you.

Then, there were the days when you worked just as hard at putting a decent case together, and you made the mistake of informing the victims that you felt confident that it was all wrapped up, essentially delivered with a bow. Later, you find out that your charges were dumped in favor of a plea deal for a reduced charge because the suspect pled to a much less significant case from another agency. You soon find yourself delivering the bad news to those same victims.

"We almost had this one, I'm sorry. He is pleading to two charges, but several of the other charges were dropped. Our case was unfortunately one of them."

A few weeks later, you see the suspect from the case walking around town. He gives you the finger and then giggles like a delighted schoolboy.

You begin to go fishing more, and you tend to put your phone on silent when it should be answered with the eagerness of an eight-year-old who was invited to a birthday party at a house with an in-ground pool—you just don't feel like swimming anymore.

I digress.

One night—thirty years in—you open your email to find a note from a kid you treated well in his wilding phase. He spiraled downward after he got into the heroin, and he did things that both of you never thought possible.

When he pulled a late-night armed robbery and ran for three days while you tried to bring him in, you figured he was going to end up dead because of his reckless and dangerous choices.

When he gives up and comes out of his hiding place, he says things to you that are threatening, hateful, and clearly driven by his addiction. It still makes you wonder where that good kid had gone. You know he is in there somewhere, but it becomes effortless to feel like it's okay to hate him back. Almost.

This note, from my email:

> On 12-26-11, you arrested me in Veazie, Maine, and that day would change my life forever.
>
> I was very messed up into drugs, and the way you talked to me put my life into a spin after that day. I never went back to using again. I went to jail—this time with a different attitude, one that wanted a life back.
>
> I got sentenced to three years in prison, did my time, took classes, helped teach auto body, worked, and stayed to myself.

I got out and left for Texas. I worked there for four years till I was ready, then came home to my family, and I've never looked back. I have an amazing girl, we have amazing children, and I have an amazing job, a nice place, a car, and I push myself to do even better every day. So, I just wanted to say thank you, sir.

Yours truly,
J. D.

My advice to any young cop is to cling to the right end of the almost and be patient. Be very, very patient.

COMFORTABLE

THE COMFORT LEVEL OF A TINY CABIN COMES FROM THE CENtered and settled feelings that envelop one's inner self when the key is turned in the old, tarnished knob upon your return.

Building small was intentional, as I am a horrible entertainer. As time flies by—and you know it does—even minor expansions of the family make the old place shrink like cotton left too long in the dryer.

When I land here—only with Ellie—the innkeeper determines the sleeping arrangements; my choice is the one that is typically the most uncomfortable. I can't answer why that is, however.

I have a soft twin bed—slung from four manila ropes—that hangs from the ceiling of the screened-in porch. When the rare company shows up, I offer that up to them first. It's an experience that needs to be checked off the list of a foreigner to the woods and lake.

I think it's the wanderings and wonderings of the mind as you hear Maine critters moving about in the night while you are covered in the thick ink of misty darkness. With only screens for "protection," it can be a little uncomfortable if you don't fully understand that fur-covered quadrupeds don't really have any desire to get inside. There is some height to the porch; critters would first have to climb a few feet in order to access your dreams. None of them do.

The most commonly held horror stories of the woods include bears; they are here, but they don't seek out flatlanders who swing and sway themselves to sleep on the porch.

I should add that while I have described the porch-sleeping experience quite clearly, I don't sleep out there as much as I used to. I save the first porch sleeping experience of the season for my significant other. She's not commonly in the same zip code as I am, but on her last visit, I offered to make up the bed behind the screens. She declined.

It was forecast to be thirty degrees that night, and while that is close to the optimum temperature for infesting a warm sleeping bag with your soul, she said that she would wait until her return, later in the summer. I am leaving the "first sleep" for her.

So, the lonely bed still swings to the breeze while hoping for company—I mean, other than Ellie. She utilizes the bed for afternoon naps, and I let her. The sun strikes the center of the mattress at just the perfect angle for drying out lake-dampened black fur.

As for me? I still sleep on the pull-out couch that—when opened—centers in front of the sliding glass and screen doors to the porch. I leave the glass pulled aside, and when there are no mosquitoes to speak of on the interior perimeter of the porch, I pull back the sliding screen door, too.

It's an uncomfortable bed, and my back is a little sore in the morning from my toss-and-turn sleeping style. I most enjoy the slightly muffled noises from outside during the night.

The breeze flows over the bed, and that makes an extra blanket a treasured cohost when pulled to the chin in the black of a moonless night.

The back pain subsides quickly once I walk outside to the luxurious bathroom accommodations on the wooded hill. I stretch and groan a little as I walk the path. I heard the noise keeps the black bears away.

I don't come here to be comfortable. I come here to feel comfortable; there is a difference.

COTTER PIN

I WAS CRANKING BEN RECTOR'S MUSIC AND MOWING AT A speed that can be reconciled only by the rate at which the storm clouds were approaching.

The old John Deere just ain't what she used to be, and, amid some high-speed turns, I noted that the mowing deck had been taken advantage of by old age, gravity, and a suddenly missing cotter pin; I had made furrows where there once were none.

I dismounted and stared at the mower for a few moments. One of my go-to repair strategies is to stare at things. Staring is made more fruitful and relaxing by listening to a musical soundtrack.

I concluded that I had never removed the mowing deck from the tractor because there had been no need. It had been running perfectly ever since I had reallocated the contraption— at a righteous price—from its third owner.

As I stretched out on the ground beside the machine, I determined that it was fortuitous that I had transitioned back to the medium ear-canal inserts on my Air Pods. Three different sizes of white rubber ductwork come included—standard—in every box of pods.

Since there is no hygienic way to determine the proper size of your own ear canals, I started off with the largest size. I firmly believed that there must be some basis for the unkind jokes from fellow fifth graders so many years ago.

I noted that I continually had to push them back in whenever I exuded the slightest bit of perspiration. Ear sweat is not something that we like to talk about, but it's real, and it's a problem when using the wrong rubber ductwork from the selections that Apple provides.

The new configuration allowed me to lie in the grass and ponder my plight while still being calmed by the soothing tones of Ben Rector. It's not a big thing, but I must tell you that being bothered by only one of the two problems at hand has a way of making both minor in the scheme of a poorly planned and executed, high-speed lawn-mowing event.

Instead of pushing the sound-makers back into my—only recently discovered—smaller ear canals, I merely had to let the music continue playing and stare at the problem until I figured out that something was missing in my life. In this case, it was a cotter pin.

I crawled to the opposite side of the lawn tractor to investigate whether this might be a situation where both sides are connected the same way. If so, it would help me avoid searching Google for "John Deere mowing deck won't return to the original position by pulling up on handle on the left side of the seat." Much to my satisfaction, the opposite side of the tractor still had all the parts attached. It appeared to be a mirror image of the left side.

Now, mind you, I was still listening to Ben Rector's album, *Magic*. It came out in 2018. I brushed off the grassy fodder from the escapade of resentful and recumbent review, and then I wandered into the house.

About a year ago, at an impromptu garage sale, I purchased two Craftsman toolboxes from a guy who had been kicked out of his house one night when he returned home a little too early from a business trip.

It's not my place to share any more detail about that, but you should know that he and his soon-to-be ex-wife quickly came to an understanding that he should have called first.

This unfortunate event landed me in another one of those uncomfortable positions; it was much more painful than lying on the ground staring at the mowing deck. In the end, the prices were agreed upon, and I bought the two rolling boxes and all the contents. I then skedaddled from the property before the discord became more palpable. It felt a bit odd to be an unwilling participant in the delicate discount ballet that *is* a garage sale for a couple during a nasty divorce.

I dug around in box number one and found some mechanic's wire that I felt could be fashioned into a proper "latch" to hold me over. I then excavated a bit, deep into the bottom drawer of cabinet number two. I found a package of two cotter pins in a plastic bag; the bag was marked "John Deere" in freehand Sharpie.

I grabbed one of the pins, a pair of pliers—just in case this wasn't magic—and walked back out to the tractor. The cotter pin was an exact match for the missing pin.

I reattached the mowing deck, adjusted the volume to the *Magic* album, and started the old girl back up. My repair job was completed before the showers came, and I never once had to push the Air Pods back into my—now determined to be dainty—ear canals.

That's when the song "Boxes" came on. I had never heard it before that fateful day. Yes, I found it odd too, but everything happens for a reason.

In a short period, I learned that there are days when it's better to arrive home a little late; garage sales can be worth your time even if you don't know what you are looking for; music can become an ironic soundtrack at end-of-day events; and it took me fifty-seven years to realize that my ears are not as big as the other kids used to tell me they were.

Drafty Windows and a Dog Named Jack

My first home was built in 1865; it was about 100 years old when I was born and aged gracefully while I grew up. The deed became mine when I was in my mid-twenties. I always told people the place had been used—a lot.

We bought it in the fall of the year; the only heat source was burning wood. Two cast iron Vermont Castings stoves belted out a creaking, crackling song as hardwood became smoke, ember, and ash.

The wind whistled through the loose panes of the old windows as the sparsely insulated walls gave those stoves all the oxygen they needed for a good burn. Strategic sitting was required to avoid a draft on your neck or your ankles, usually at the same time.

I was young, broke, dumb, and happy.

My lady-friend, later to be called Mrs. Cotton, was a scavenger of formerly well-loved furniture. She found a decent used couch and chair; both were uncomfortable.

She was finishing her degree and stopped by from time to time to replenish the bare cupboards or throw up an antique mirror or three that she found at yard sales. She loved to reflect on a bargain. Some of those mirrors were later found to be valuable. She had a good eye for everything but men. God bless her.

I didn't care; having all the lovely mirrors with minimal furniture to block the reflections allowed me an unimpeded view of the off-white lace curtains dancing smartly in other rooms as the wind blew right through the ancient plaster and lath walls.

Winter nights, like tonight, were blistering cold in the old place, and I had a regimen of adding wood to one of the two stoves about every two and a half hours. This method gave each stove about a five-hour burn time. I had one in the living room and one in the dining room, no more than twenty feet apart. I slept on a mattress on the floor in the corner of the dining room. I call it the dining room, but there was no dining table in the room for a considerable amount of time. This—in truth—must have made it a bedroom.

I had shut off the upstairs for the winter because, well, there was no reason to add the stress of running up and down the stairs to attend to the endless stoking of the stoves.

My companion on those nights was a black and white Redbone hound-Labrador mix named Jackson. I picked him up at the mall, back when people would sometimes bring a pen full of puppies to the center court to sell. These were not puppy-mill puppies; they were inadvertently bred farm mutts. I use the word "mutt" with full respect to Jack's parents.

I paid five dollars for the boy. Abe Lincoln never made a better deal.

Yes, his name was Jackson Lab—in a homage to the famous Bar Harbor genetic research facility where fine white mice are raised and studied. The name made me laugh, and it stuck.

He was loyal and a fierce watchdog. His eighty-pound body was a welcome bed warmer for those nights when I stretched the stoking times to three hours.

For a long time, there was no operational lock on the kitchen door, and I never worried—not even once—about the possibility of a burglary. For one thing, I owned nothing but a mattress, a few mirrors, and lovely lace curtains.

Secondly, that kind and loving animal turned into the Tasmanian devil when folks tried to enter his turf. Any burglar who was worthy of the moniker would have been easy to catch on the way out. They would have been easily followed in a light tracking snow due to the guaranteed loss of body fluids of one type or another after encountering Jack.

Jack kept me safe and warm as the curtains moved like tethered ghosts in the darkness while cast-iron wood stoves groaned under constant expansion and contraction. He snored, and I think I did too; neither of us complained.

I would listen to the wind on those nights, wondering when I would have the money for new windows or when I might afford to add a furnace to the antique cape. Those needs were eventually met, and Jack was rewarded for his hardships with a new king-size mattress and the eventual arrival of Mrs. Cotton.

Jack's been gone about twenty-one years this winter.

You always want more when you have less, and while it's a worthy pursuit to aim toward lofty goals or to strive to have better things, you'd never have appreciated even one of them if it weren't for the leaner times, or for those who shared them with you.

Tonight, the same wind blows cold snow over the top of a warmer home with far fewer cracks and much better windows, and here I am just wondering how Jack is.

Driving Barefoot: The Eighth Deadly Sin?

If you are the child of a parent who made it a point to tell you that driving barefooted is against the law, prepare for redemption.

If you are a parent telling your offspring that it is illegal to operate a motor vehicle in a shoeless state, barefooted, sans-shoes, or while wearing flip-flops or another type of non-structured footwear, keep this posting away from the children.

Can a person legally drive a vehicle while barefooted? The answer is yes.

As a police officer, I cannot count the number of times that this question has been posed to me over the years. Typically, by a teenager and usually in front of their parents. That puts a lot of pressure on a cop. I am a parent, but I never told my son this lie. I am not a helicopter parent.

Living in Maine, our window of opportunity for shoe-less driving is short. I never even thought about talking to him about it. Flip-flops in our house are reserved by the door for taking the dog outside. When you have dogs, walkabouts without shoes are not a great idea.

When asked this question, I know that I have just been drafted as a pawn in the teen's game of calling out the parents for a suspected lie. I work quickly to change the subject or avoid directly answering the question.

I might say something like, "I can tell you this: driving without wearing shoes is not a great idea." Maybe, if I were going for supportive parent mode, I would blurt this out, "I fully believe if your parents don't think that is a safe practice, you should avoid it at all costs." This would not be a lie, as I think parental advice is a good thing, and sometimes we do know better.

This perception that it is illegal to drive without shoes started somewhere back in time. Probably before our ability to double-check facts through search engines. Some parents started this rumor, and it stuck. It carried through the 1960s and into the 1990s. The kids began to get cynical and finally began researching the subject. The jig is up, people. It is time to explain to the kids why you lied. When Google sits in the second chair beside the teen debate champ, you might have your work cut out for you.

I did a post on our department's Facebook page that clarified and verified that driving with "nekkid feet" was not against the law in any state in the United States. It was well-received, and even though I believed that most adults among us would have Googled the laws nationwide by now, many still do not know that the practice was, and is, legal. How does this happen in the age of instant information?

The comments we received were much more humorous than the lighthearted post I created. I had people sharing it repeatedly, and some jubilant drivers claimed that they were throwing their shoes out the window that very moment. I don't support this behavior for many reasons, but now is not the time for a post about littering. Plus, shoes are expensive.

Several motor vehicle operators wrote to me about the shame they felt when they defied both their parents and the nonexistent worldwide edict that shoeless pedal manipulation was illegal. Some believed it to be a mortal sin against humanity. Imagine when the veil was lifted, and they came to the realization that this was just driving without shoes. In other words, just driving.

I did get a scathing review from one individual. The man indicated that he could not believe that I did not understand the laws about due regard for the safe operation of a motor vehicle and that I could and should write a summons to a driver who chose to operate in the unshod mode. He also made it clear that I should be ashamed. Vehement and displeased, he gave us a one-star rating.

I have been doing police work for a very long time, and never had I been dressed down so angrily over failing to ticket someone for not breaking the law. It was always frowned upon by the higher-ups.

I pose this question: How do we make other, existing laws become this ingrained in folks' heads?

Texting and driving are spoken about repeatedly. I see, hear, and read the public service announcements daily. We send out details of police officers with the intent to stop and warn or summons people for the behavior. Then I drive home and watch at least a third of the drivers on the road text like it is a necessary part of the operation of their motor vehicles.

We need to find out the person who started the rumor about driving barefoot and have them work this issue into their indoctrination speech.

Personally, I am not sure that expensive fines stop an activity that happens at dinner, bath time, at the movies, and pretty much whenever I am talking to someone. Most people I encounter don't give a second thought about stopping our colloquy to pull up their phone and respond to something that appears on their screen.

The sad thing is that it is not even against the law to operate a motorcycle without shoes. At least in forty-nine states. Don't kick the messenger. It is true. Alabama does appear to have a law that prohibits such activity.

I assumed that some location on the West Coast would be more inclined to disallow operating a motorcycle without all the gear all the time. Let me be clear: I do not believe that using a bike without footwear is safe. I would not do it, and you probably shouldn't either.

So, there are no laws that disallow free-footed-pedal-fondling tomfoolery, and there really shouldn't be. Let me know if you come up with an idea of creating some fear and paranoia about distracted driving and texting while behind the wheel. You know, something that *is* against the law.

If you come up with something, text me. You don't even need to be wearing flip-flops.

Dumped Dawn

I don't know why it upset me so much, but it did.

I was the one who stepped up and purchased the largest container possible. We went to the big box store on one of her visits to our home. You know the one; everything is super-sized. Just when you think they can't make a product any larger, someone wraps plastic around two or three of whatever you don't need so that you can carry home too much of it.

This was the Platinum Edition of the Dawn dish detergent—it has (or had) four times the cleaning power. I don't know who rates it platinum, but I bought it. It appears that Dawn's marketing team is on to something.

The oversized vessel of all that is soon to be greaseless was clearly intended to be utilized to fill smaller vessels. It should have been stored under the sink, but I was happy to place it on the windowsill. I like to see the sun shining through the cobalt blue liquid.

She put it away—fittingly—before she left. But I put it right back on the sill after she zipped off to the places she wanders.

Focusing only on the mechanics of it all, I found there was no need to bend over and reach deep into the already cramped cabinet each time I wanted to wash a couple of bowls and three spoons. For the record, the extra spoon comes from being utilized to deliver a dollop of peanut butter to Ellie. The dog immediately rushes to the sound of any plastic lid being spun upward, and hopefully, off.

While walking into the house in the late afternoon, the sun shines through the thick liquid detergent. It creates a pleasant azure hue on the adjacent countertop. I know, admitting to such frivolity causes you to confirm that I am a simple guy, and indeed I am.

I do the dishes quickly, but they sit in the second stainless sink for about three to five days. I have plenty more in the cupboard, and when the double sink is full of cleansed and air-dried dishes, I return them to their comfortable locations in the cluttered cabinets.

One night, I must have bumped the bottle when pulling the drapes closed for my imminent slumber. The cotton curtains seem to redirect some of the drafts that inevitably sneak into the house when the north wind shows up in a minor rage.

The next day, I discovered that the jug had fallen over sometime overnight. A pleasantly plaid dishtowel—draped over the well-drained dishes—must have muffled the impact as the bottle ended up, pointed down, with the cap opened. A small stack of bowls acted as a fulcrum for the bottle and aided the direct flow of Dawn down the drain and to the distantly attached septic tank.

I was crestfallen. This bottle could have easily lasted for three or four more years.

The bottle was not completely drained, and I probably will have enough Dawn to do dishes until the point when I return to the grocery store to buy a smaller bottle. I was not a good steward of the Platinum Jug, and I don't deserve that much Dawn. Maybe no one does.

What bothers me most is that the loss of the Dawn bothers me at all. I can afford another bottle due to my current state of employment. For some reason, the king-sized container with copious amounts of cobalt cleanser brought me joy—which, incidentally, was the same dish detergent that my grandmother used when I was a kid; of course, she kept it under the sink.

I have learned a valuable lesson—things are often darkest after you dump the Dawn.

ELLIE IN THE RAIN

IT'S NOT OFTEN THAT I GO OUTSIDE AND FIND MYSELF fearful—last night was a little different. After the heavy snow of last week left many powerless and with a plethora of downed trees, I noted several widow-makers hanging up in a couple of the hardwood trees that stand on the edge of my dooryard.

During daylight hours, I made a note to myself about where the more ominous broken branches were hanging—by the last fiber of their being—and I avoided standing or walking anywhere near them. I'd get them pulled down but not for a few weeks.

Last night's evening jaunt with the dog found me staying a little closer to the house as the wind had picked up with reported gusts of sixty miles per hour. Indeed, not all the wind was traveling the speed limit, but it was a steady and unseen forty-plus swaying the maples like a meadow full of spring flowers. I listened for the telltale sign of the broken branches losing their grip and beginning an unplanned descent.

It was pitch black—raining hard and horizontal—as I waited for Ellie to return from the woods where she reliably leaves all that is unneeded on a very regular basis. Hollering out of frustration—and a slight fear of walking toward her last suspected location—I yelled a little louder for her. She didn't come.

Knowing the roar of the wind coupled with the rhythm of driving rain was probably muffling my yelps, I waited under an eave of the house to try to stay dry enough only to be mad about her lack of speed at doing her deeds.

After about two minutes, I became concerned and walked down into the wood line to see what was happening; I couldn't find her.

Upon my return to the shadows of the eaves, I discovered that Ellie had not left the protection of the overhang. There she sat—watching me—while I was looking for her. Her head was dry as a bone. It became clear that she had never left the protection of the eaves as she sat silently watching me as I hollered—out of concern—for her.

My significant other had selected Ellie from a batch of multicolored puppies. She loved the sheen of her black coat. On the way home with the puppy, I mentioned that I had become accustomed to having a predominantly white dog for the prior fifteen years. My glee—partly—was because of my ability to pick him out in the darkness during nighttime wanderings.

I laughed through gritted teeth at Ellie's dainty decision to keep her fur dry rather than showing any concern about her internal water content.

I scolded her as kindly as I could to goad her into leaving the relative safety of our spot. It took verbal provocation and a pull/push on her collar to get her to move into that flailing forest canopy that shelters the sacred pooping grounds. She was not happy, but neither was I.

She finally wedged herself into a spot that she considered reasonable, finished strong, and sprinted back toward the house. I caught up while she stared back at me from an overhang on the porch.

Once inside, she barely had to shake off the residual water while I shook my coat outside the door to drain it from our jaunt. I think she most enjoyed the unplanned swapping of our nightly roles.

February Sun

In February, it's the sun that is the headliner.

Sure, you notice the patches of ice, the crystallized, granulated goodness of snow that changes consistency on an hourly basis, and the lack of foliage on your—all bark with no bite—deciduously inclined lawn ornaments. But it's the warmth of the sun that sets February apart from the other winter months.

It's all about science and angles, but as we lumber toward the March equinox, the sun begins to glance off your face in a manner that is much more welcoming than it was in December and January.

It's much like the fourth date with the shy lass from your sophomore year. Four dates meant that at least four Fridays had passed since the flirtatious locker-side chats turned to the full-on feeling of "This must be love, but if it isn't, it sure ain't bad." Maybe the relationship had turned the corner, and you were coming up on, "I should surely take this lady to the Dairy Queen on two-for-one brazier burger night; I'll skip the chili dogs for this woman."

In our current communicative state, the excessive texting and ridiculously overused emojis would have turned the relationship sour in half that time; the February sun is a far more reliable way to warm your cold winter bones. It comes on slow and strong.

I would have made the connection to brewing a good cup of coffee, but the angle of the sun made me consider how I have loved the feeling of a sunbeam on my face since long before my sophomore year, and it's even more welcome now. I make far too many coffee analogies already.

I enjoyed growing up in a slower time. I appreciated the personal relationship that I built with the seasonal changes, even while ignoring the scientific reasons for them.

And what pleasant and shy lass wouldn't want to be compared to the warmth that's provided by a sunny February day? Probably most of them, but most are not all, and that suits me just fine. I'll stand in the sun today.

Flat Tractor Tire—
Spring Chores with a Side of Snow

Our futile attempt to shed the heavy cloak of winter and embrace the opportunity to squeeze a few chores into the small—black-fly free—window that allows spring breezes to blow the dust from our currently shuttered lives is slowed by the remaining snow on the ground. And the longer-range forecast calls for more snow tomorrow.

It won't last, or "stick," as the old men say while leaning on tailgates outside the corner store. Still, it is a kick in the nuggets when you are hoping for a few dry spots that will allow you to avoid mud while walking across the lawn or dooryard.

I was on my game this weekend; my son and I tenuously fixed a flat tire on the front of the tractor in preparation for dragging the ruts out of the camp road. The tire held air, but we looked at each other with eyebrows raised in suspicious synchronicity, typically reserved for only The Police.

The plug did not bore far enough into the carcass of the agricultural-treaded Goodyear. The nail we dug out had no trouble diving into the center of the tire, but the plug was stubborn on its descent into the vast void of stale air. Still, it appeared to no longer be leaking. I could tell by the scientific searching for the bubbling of the self-applied saliva that I lovingly dabbed around the hole. If that grosses you out, I understand, but no one has time to grab a spray bottle of soapy water when the sun is going down a bit faster than the height of an old tractor tire.

We both slapped the tire as if we were congratulating it for graduating from college. The friendly ringing that emanates from an adequately inflated tire was our reward for a job partially done.

It went flat two hours into the three-hour job. I got just enough gravel moved so that the ruts were smoothed nicely, but there are still piles of rocks and debris that will be smothered and soaked by tomorrow's snow event. I'd get to it, but first, I needed to plug the tire again.

That only comes after hauling the implement back home on a flatbed trailer that, for some reason, eliminates much gasoline from the tank of the truck. The good news is that gas was cheap right then. I'd gladly pay more for it if there were more places to go, but it still is nice to pay half price to go nowhere in particular.

One step forward, one-and-a-quarter steps back; that's spring in Maine—spring 2021, the year of our COVID.

FOG

THE MISTY GRAY GHOST MADE UP OF WELL-SUSPENDED MI-croscopic specks of dreary droplets has a way of suppressing long-distance vision.

Fog makes it acceptable—and comfortable—to look a little closer at the sights and sounds that surround you. You might have ignored them if not for being draped in the cooling cloak of untouchable vapor.

Fog allows a more focused approach to your next step and washes away some of the worries that often accompany a long-term plan.

Fog cannot be trusted, but it forces you to trust yourself.

Get a Robe

Temperatures in the high thirties led me to settle down on an ice-free spot on the wooden steps. It always feels good to sit in a sunbeam.

I pondered several things, including how the heck the Chewy-dot-com order of forty pounds of dog food had arrived less than twenty-four hours after I placed my order; I saw the distinctly marked box sitting in a receding snowbank.

The FedEx guy put it under an overhanging eave of the house to avoid a waterfall of melting snow from soaking through the box before I made the discovery that it had arrived.

That must have been why Ellie went ballistic while I was in the shower, scrubbing down the broken-down machine that is TC. It was full demon-mode.

It's disconcerting to be standing behind a curtain under a stream of hot water when the dog pulls a nutty because some uninvited company has arrived. You wonder if it's a guest, even though you never have guests beyond close family.

Could it be that it's someone with ill-intent? My level of worry doesn't move the gauge. The dog is loud; devices designed to rid the property of unwanted vermin are readily available.

I am not a man who enjoys violence, but if you get by the dog, I stand ready to snap you with a towel. More dangerous types would have to deal with the Louisville Slugger signed by the entire 2004 World Series-winning Red Sox team.

My son has a key, so I have been surprised before. I heard no one knock; if I had, I know the distinct sound of Ellie bouncing off the steel entry door.

It can be surprising to wander out of the shower with no previous concerns about someone being in the house, only to find that someone has made their way into the house. Especially if you are nekkid. The exit from the rain-locker room is a sharp left turn to my bedroom. A full-frontal presentation to visitors in the living room would necessitate a right turn.

In other words, any pleasantly comfortable company would probably get a glimpse of something uncomfortable but not all that disturbing. It's not like you cannot find this view on late-night network television; I usually go directly to the bedroom when looking for raiment. I really should get a robe.

No worries, it was just a dog food delivery. Ellie seemed relieved as she sniffed the box while I sat facing the sunbeam. Yup, I dressed before going outside. She has no idea how easy her life is, other than I don't have a proper robe.

Goose Poo

I'M NOT TALKING ABOUT A COUPLE OF PILES OF GOOSE POO; this was an apparent land assault that rivaled the invasion of Normandy.

What's good for the goose—and gander—is not good for those who wander . . . barefooted around the property.

I was not aware of the leavings in the front (and back) of the camp. I came in very late at night, but in early-morning briefings with Paul and Shirley, I was apprised that their shore-front had been invaded by an entire squadron of geese with a bad case of the s@%&s. I laughed because I was in their quiet spot; I had not checked mine.

What is sad is that the feathered Canadas came for the hostas. It's usually the deer that clean off the few flowering plants that grow—well—around here. Paul showed me where the plants had been ripped up by the beaks of the winged beasts.

I have a few hostas planted around the camp, but I found upon my return to the cabin that these webbed warriors had marched inland, mining the lawn with scat that rivals—in size—piles that could have been left behind by invading Great Danes (the dogs, not the warriors). I've seen goose poo, but I have never experienced the volume of formerly flying fecal matter that was left on the lawn.

In a moment of peaceful reflection, I began to count the piles as I walked back up the hill to take cover. This seems like a waste of time, but I had to look down while walking to avoid embedding the remnants of the all-you-can-eat Canadian-attended buffet that was consumed by the flock. In one hundred feet, give or take, I counted twenty-three distinct and specific relief zones. If I had cast my eyes in a wider pattern, one can assume I would have counted triple that in goose leavings. These are piles that would make a bowel-affected Pomeranian proud.

Yeah, I know it's not a Sunday morning brunch-worthy conversation, but I was preparing to power weed-trim the front lot with a gas weed whacker. I needed to find some old ski goggles and a pair of higher Red Wings to keep from getting scat flashbacks, later.

I even found three piles *under* the boat and trailer. Any respectable goose would have had to duck (see what I did there?) under the boat to relieve themselves. It was obvious that a full (now empty) regiment had shown up.

Even if I had been here, I guess I would have merely surrendered to their number two tactics. I'm still glad I missed it.

I can only hope that when they pulled out, their takeoff demanded far less distance to become airborne. Then again, there are probably a few leavings on the roof, but I'm not going to check.

I need breakfast.

Horace was Wrong

According to Ellie's pedometer, we covered well over four hundred miles yesterday. We left for Portland, Maine, at 0558 hours, recorded the last chapter of the book for Audible, turned north to return to the Bangor region by 1730 hours.

The adult in me demanded twenty minutes on the couch for what I believed would be a nap, but it didn't happen. Wading through the grass to enter the house reminded me that rain had fallen, and subsequent weeds—from a distance appearing like grass—had reached critical mass.

I plugged in the ear pods and mowed down various grasses and weeds that come preplanted in any load of Maine loam (pronounced "loom" here). I returned to the house and pondered whether I wanted to get on the road to the woods.

There was still enough daylight to cause me to believe that I would make it halfway to camp before I needed to start squinting at roadside shadows in preparation for a darting moose. Yes, they lumber, but sometimes they dart.

Darting moose can cause denting and, sometimes, death; dang it.

I grabbed the two preloaded camp bags that portray the embroidered initials of a man or woman I had never met. You see, the secret of getting a terrific deal on a dark green canvas zip-top tote bag from L.L.Bean is to find a returned sack that someone—somewhere—found to be unacceptable; I have a matching set.

The bags are the same color, but they have two different initials. I have always believed if I were to take up with the naughty task of smuggling things that were deemed illegal, I could be reasonably believable in my plea that the bags did not belong to me. I'd still fail because I smirk when I fib—ask my mom.

In the future, remind me to share with you how many in-correctly monogrammed Bean's dress shirts I own. That has caused several confusing conversations.

I digress.

We loaded up, grabbed a ladder from the backyard to achieve lofty goals in the area where squirrels had been entering, and we zipped to the fuel stop. I purchased a horrible two-day-old sandwich, thirty gallons of petrol, and a tall cup of black Guatemalan driving juice.

Ellie loved the second half of the egg salad; I felt we should do it as a team if we were going to become ill.

We took "The Airline," as the road is a straight shot to Canada. Sure, I turn right a reasonable distance before we start hearing kind comments from border guards, but it's the best way to go—except after dark. The moose? They dart.

I added all the voltage allowable by law to the headlights, and we motivated east while being fueled by two-dollar gas, two-day-old mayonnaise, and dreams of sleeping where the breezes drag Atlantic air across our food-poisoned bodies.

We saw two moose lumbering to our right, three deer, a handsome raccoon, and one fox. We met—incidentally—three million suicidal insects whose main goal was to destroy the sloppy wax job I had applied to the grill of the truck to aid in washing away their memory and their cadavers.

We enjoyed watching the sun tuck in for the night from our rolling vantage point. I love heading for the coast and the woods.

Horace Greely had it all wrong—I say, head east, old man, head east.

I Stood Back

I stood back. COVID, you know.

The older man was clad in wrinkled khakis, a cracked brown faux leather alligator belt with a tarnished buckle, and old shoes; his coat looked like it was warm.

His silver metal-framed eyeglasses showed signs of unsuccessful attempts at home repair. Tape filled the gaps where bending—one too many times—had caused a weakness in the structure. The lenses were visibly scratched.

New eyeglasses are expensive. I hadn't thought much about it right up until then. I needed to replace my own at some point soon.

Each morning, when I pick up my glasses from wherever I thought I had lost them the night before, I can see the scratches as I raise them to my face.

Once they settle in on the bridge of my nose, my eyes automatically make the necessary accommodations, and the view through the lenses is fine for another day.

I bet he feels the same way. The adage that "this (or these) works just fine" was probably one of his mantras.

Even as I describe him, I'd say he brought the whole ensemble together nicely. The sum of our parts, even when well worn, can still have an overall pleasant appearance. He had pulled it off.

He gazed at the pastries, then he asked about the chocolate brownies. He was bent over, peering right at them. They were huge.

He put his finger on the glass, pointing at one. It didn't appear that anyone was paying attention to him. It was more than likely because the place was so busy.

I could see his pointing finger was a part of his decision-making process. He had time; no one was waiting for him at home, I could tell.

He moved his finger up the rounded glass display case. Dragging it along the radius of the smooth protective shield, he settled on one of the cakes. It was about three rows back from the front. That's the one I would have selected as well. It was a bit bigger than the others. He looked down his finger as if he were setting up the sights on a rifle for the perfect shot. He selected his quarry.

I'm a pretty good judge of age, but I didn't try to guess his. I was too busy trying to figure out exactly why this brownie, this post-dinner delight, was so important to him. And, yes, he was holding up the line. I stopped worrying if my pick-up order was getting cold when I started watching him.

Internally, I hoped he would stay all day; I was rooting for him. I wanted that brownie to be the best one that he ever tasted.

When the busy lady at the counter turned her attention toward him, he pulled the trigger. His finger stayed right on the glass. He aimed it well enough that she was able to select—and pluck—his brownie right out of the case. "That's the one," he said.

He paralleled her walk down the counter to the cash register. He didn't get there as fast as she did. It took him a while to straighten up, get out his tattered wallet, and select a few dollars from between the scraps of paper he was saving inside the compartment.

He knew the cost, and he presented her his cash. She bagged it up and placed it on the counter.

He grasped the bag only after reconfiguring the papers that tried to come out of his wallet when he retrieved the dollar bills. The wallet slid easily back into the back pocket of his baggy khakis.

He said, "I wonder if it will be as good as the brownies my mother used to make." And with that, he slowly walked out in the bright sunshine of another brisk January day.

I mentally crossed my fingers that the brownie would hit the spot. I knew it wouldn't. It's challenging to hit the target when it's so far behind you.

The clearer picture sometimes demands that we stand back for a time.

COVID, you know.

Jesus Take the Wheel

I WANT TO DRIVE MY OWN CAR. I HAVE NO DESIRE TO LET computers and sensors decide on the line my car should take on the way to my destination.

You can argue that computers and sensors are already in control of the engine and other onboard systems, but I am still steering and braking; at least, I think I am. I would like to keep it that way.

There have been a few tragedies involving self-driving automobiles; I am not writing to criticize the technology. I know very little about the nuts and bolts of the system, or should I say, the lack of nuts and bolts in the technology. I am basing my opinion on the fact that I know enough about human beings behind the wheel that I do not believe this is a good idea. Not even for a short stint of "mascara time." I should stop using it anyway. It does irritate my skin.

It is apparent that the drivers of some of those cars did not follow the manufacturer's instructions that both hands remain on the wheel. I believe the driver should be prepared to steer if it becomes necessary.

Even keeping a knee on the wheel would be far better than letting go entirely. I am not endorsing using a knee to do the job of your hands, but it certainly would be better than complete disengagement from the process.

Knee driving is an art that I learned while cruising with my dad in each one of his many, many Chevrolets. My dad's name is Art. Coincidence? I think not.

Dad held several jobs; he was a minister and an insurance salesman. The insurance sales paid the bills that the church could not. As I got older, I realized that my dad had all the bases covered. Prayer was good, but why not guarantee that you will collect a pittance for your injury if the prayer did not take. "God works in mysterious ways" was not a sales pitch as much as it was the truth when you fell off the ladder.

One such blessing of this arrangement was that you could contact your clergy and claims manager in the same phone call.

The visit from your minister could include a claims check as well as an opportunity to renew your policy. Indeed, there is no charge for divine intervention.

I would go with him on occasion and wait in the car during sales calls. There was no air-conditioning in our vehicles, so the windows were rolled down. Pop always left the key in the ignition, so I was entertained by the AM Delco. Audiovox FM converters came much later.

I used to watch my father avoid angry dogs and angry people. He would sometimes end up bringing fresh baked cookies back to the car for the kid (me) who was either sweating or freezing (in the case of Christmas vacation sales trips). I made sure that I would be visible to anyone in the house by putting on my hungry face. It worked from time to time.

Between stops, fast food was the chosen fare, and Art could pound a quarter pounder and eat fries with a fluidity I could never imitate. He could steer with his left knee while smoothly operating the brake and gas pedal with the illusion that he was using his hands. Well, he was using his hands but not for steering. No Cokes were spilled in the making of my summer memories riding around the back roads of Maine.

I became a darn good knee driver as time went on. It is doubtful that the next generation of programming will urge the operator to always keep one knee on the wheel while the self-driving mode is engaged. Still, it seems like it is a better arrangement than no connection.

The slippery slope of self-driving cars is that humans always take it to the next level. Typically, that level is below the first. People have a way of wrecking everything, including their automobiles.

Placing the car on autopilot to eat a sandwich seems a reasonable use for the system. However, eating a sandwich will give way to making a sandwich. It won't be long before drivers want to make a loaf of bread. Possibly churning their own butter on straight stretches.

The motor vehicle operators who read books, newspapers, and magazines while driving will become writers. This will lead to a craze in mobile publishing ventures. Meetings over the latest manuscript will take place in the backseat. Fresh bread will be served.

The concept is terrific, but if you give a driver the ability to totally relax behind the wheel, they will. Things could get worse if the technology makes its way to other cars.

Live reviews of automobiles done by drivers (who should be driving) will hit the Facebook feeds. Other drivers will be watching them, hitting likes, hearts, and angry face emojis while they take a break from the daily commute. Chaos will ensue.

The game of punch-buggy will become a contact sport with the driver being fully involved. Outweighing the offspring by a good one hundred pounds will make the simple, time-tested game of just passing the time into a painful proposition.

When Dad comes over the front-seat headrest and throws junior into a headlock after passing a green 1975 Super Beetle, injuries are going to occur. The car will probably be fine for a few minutes. Still, suppose junior goes for the salt-in-eyes trick. In that case, the driver could become immobilized until an eye-wash station can be located.

The couple headed for the drive-in theater will be inclined to avoid the double-feature and just engage the self-drive mode. Letting the car travel to a selected destination will violate distracted driving laws for both the occupants and those who encounter the couple at red lights. This will cause parents with younger children to be forced to explain the ongoing situation inside the car located in the left-turn-only lane. The law of unintended consequences is an evil mistress. Shield your eyes, children. Look away.

What about families driving to Florida for their dream vacations at Disney? Suppose Dad or Mom sets the self-driving mode to take them to International Drive in Orlando. How are the kids ever going to live through the disappointment of passing by the land of plastic lizards and fireworks at South of the Border? The effect on the economy will be devastating.

There are so many tasks that I willingly will give up. Raking leaves. Washing dishes. Mowing the lawn. Shaving.

Where are the great minds that should be focusing on a lawnmower that will do the entire yard without my involvement? Doesn't that seem like a better place to start? Safeguards would need to be in place, of course. There are many places the technology should be focused on before putting other motorists' safety at risk.

Arguments can be made that this type of technology is used in air travel. I can see that. But the skies above us, as busy as they are, are wide open spaces with people on the ground watching each aircraft quite carefully. It is a different set of circumstances.

Cars are subject to encountering pedestrians, potholes, and obstacles that can enter the chosen path in an instant. Additionally, whom do you charge with operating under the influence if the driver has imbibed a little too much?

I suppose when they realize the flashing blue lights are behind them, they will need to re-engage in the driving process to pull over for their field sobriety testing.

Defense attorneys will still make billions as they pummel the cop on the stand with questions like: Did you see them driving before you stopped the vehicle? Do you know for sure that my client was not *actually* driving the car when you stopped it? The list of issues could go on forever.

I like the process of driving a car. I want to make decisions, and I want those decisions to be based on what I see in front of me. The weather conditions. The potholes in the asphalt. The volume of traffic.

I like the feeling of my rising heart rate when I am surprised by lane-changing morons and jackasses who brake at the last moment.

If I am going to crash, I want to have some input just before impact. Give me a chance for a last-ditch effort to save myself from a catastrophe. Let me experience the sole of my Red Wings slamming down the middle pedal as if it might make a difference in the outcome. I like that.

Plus, my dad prays for me daily, and he has given me a great rate on my accident policy.

Somebody get to work on that lawnmower idea. I am available for beta testing.

Just a Plastic Santa

Peering over the chipped and faded balusters surrounding the loose floorboards of a Victorian sitting porch stands a forty-six-inch-high plastic Santa Claus.

This particular Saint Nick was picked up on a whim during a late fall shopping trip to Sears and Roebuck in 1968. His bright blue eyes have seen plenty of cheer from his holiday season vantage point overlooking the corner of Lincoln Street and Farrington Avenue.

The jolly elf had missed the view during the Christmas of 1971. Ruth could not stand to be by herself and drove the Impala north to Benedicta, Maine. She wanted to be with her mother and father.

Plugging in Santa's internal electric lightbulb was a moment to savor only with her husband, Benjamin. He was probably—at that very moment—slogging through the mud in southeast Asia.

For some reason, the view of the snow-covered boulders that make up Mt. Katahdin calmed her constant fear for his safety. Ben had proposed to her on her farmhouse porch. The formidable and miles-distant Mt. Katahdin was an unapologetic witness to the whole event.

They celebrated the bliss with biscuits, woodstove-simmered baked beans, and, of course, red hot dogs.

The young couple had climbed the mountain on their honeymoon while on a camping trip at Daicy Pond. Ben claimed he could see her parents sitting on their porch—in

Benedicta—from the summit. She knew that this was not true, but the memory of his voice warmed her as the icy Aroostook County winds burned the rose color into her pale and tear-stained cheeks. She stayed at the farm through the first week of the New Year.

Plastic Santa stayed in their attic that winter. He missed the sounds of singing, the clanging of baking pans, and, of course, the voices he had come to know as a comfort to his hollow soul when they echoed upward from the floors below.

Tucked away under an eave, he never said a word; Santa understood, silently. Somehow, he knew there would be better days ahead.

The pudgy representative of the Empire Plastic Corporation returned to the porch in late November 1972, right after Thanksgiving; it was triumphant. His appearance mirrored the joyous return of Ben from Vietnam.

His now re-energized internal forty-watt bulb cast a warm glow across the lawn and to the frost-cracked sidewalk beyond. He could hear Bing Crosby belting out festive tunes from the newly purchased High-Fidelity Zenith positioned against the living room wall.

Melancholy songs were played often during Ben's absence; this music was better.

Nineteen hundred and seventy-three was a good year for some, but even better for Ruth and Ben. The impending birth announcement came in the spring. There would be twins, and certainly more if the good Lord allowed.

Each Thanksgiving, the plastic Santa emerged with a little more paint missing from his molded sack of toys. His once-bright red jacket gradually faded to pink, and his black belt became a mottled gray.

When his forty-watt heart was powered up, his twinkling blue eyes could be seen from far beyond the corner of Lincoln Street and Farrington Avenue. Even the neighbors remarked to Ruth and Ben—together and separately—that plastic Santa's eyes were a welcome sight for anyone who strolled by their home.

Ben confided that he had recently upgraded the ancient forty-watt bulb to a "brandy-new" sixty-watt incandescent bulb. But he agreed that plastic Santa's eyes were especially cheery and bright.

On his yearly journey down from the attic, plastic Santa had taken a couple of tumbles. He recovered—admirably—never letting the jolts and bumps wipe the silly grin from his round bearded face. The kids had demanded that they carry Santa down the stairway. The subsequent pushing and pulling between the siblings led to many of the jolly elf's unfortunate mishaps.

In 1979, Santa made the entire journey on his own without ever touching the stairs. After that, it was decided—in a family meeting—that his aging sense of balance was not to be tested again.

He had been teetered and tottered from the top rail of the banister too many times. Plastic Santa crashed to the birch and maple hardwood floor of the hallway below. Pride tends to go before a fall, but in this case, Santa's protruding belly struck first. The dent was pushed out after he spent some time standing beside the cast-iron steam radiator in the living room. The heat was necessary to make him more pliable for the impromptu cosmetic surgery.

"Bumbles bounce, but Santa doesn't," was not a welcome comment from Daniel. Parental smirks were quickly disguised as scowls for the sake of family unity. Plastic Santa missed the meeting. He was watching over the corner of Lincoln and

Farrington as the snow flurries, propelled by a north wind, swirled around his cheeks. He would have welcomed a chance to have input, but the last-minute gastric bypass made him far too sore to speak.

The Thanksgiving of 2013 was different. No one came to aid him on his journey down the stairs. Silently, Santa stood under the eaves expecting his ride to come.

Looking back—if a plastic Santa even has the ability to do so—he might have recalled that Ruth was thinner in 2012. She never came outside to plug in his sixty-watt lamp.

On his trip back up the stairs to the cold attic, he recalled that the decorations were not hung with the detail and attention that he had come to expect. The green and red garland that had always been lovingly wrapped around the handrail to the stairway was missing. He should have suspected something sooner.

There was a smoldering silence in the old Victorian. It was another clue that he must have missed during his standard spring and summer slumber. He was not jolted awake by visitors to the floors below, not even one time.

While he might have been cruelly described as a non-living, unknowing, and opaque Christmas representative from the Empire Plastic Corporation, it was clear to this plastic Santa that the situation was dire on the corner of Lincoln and Farrington.

All of those who might dismiss the views of the red-suited poseur would never know the situation within the house, simply because they would never take the time to ask. We all tend to ignore the obvious, especially when it feels uncomfortable.

There are some things that even a blow-molded plastic Santa can do nothing about. He missed the internal light that warmed his hollow body on cold winter nights. But, most of all, he missed his family. That, and his position overlooking the corner of Lincoln Street and Farrington Avenue.

The silent years seemed never-ending; spring and summer slumbers turned to long winter naps. The expected late autumn visitors (to his cramped and humble abode) never arrived.

In the fall of 2017, plastic Santa came to find himself in a cool basement. Wrapped in a sheet of soft plastic, his hearing was limited. His vision of the surroundings was nonexistent. Of course, he was concerned. Things had changed drastically since 1968. He had lost track of time since his separation from Ruth and Ben.

Time was lost. It was not because plastic Santa did not have a watch, clock, or calendar, but because—for a time—the memories were put on hold. Life comes with pauses that we do not control. Committing even the most insignificant moments to memory can sustain even the most stoic of cynics. Maybe Santa himself.

The voices above him sounded familiar. He could hear clanging pans, singing, and pleasantly discussed disagreements; the basement was already far better accommodations than being stuck under drafty and silent eaves. Only one floor separated him from all of the action above.

"Daniel! Where is he?"

A feminine voice had a lilt that reminded him of someone else.

"I wrapped him in bubble wrap when we moved him down from the attic. He's down in the basement."

That was Daniel's voice!

"Well, let's get him out and put him on the porch! I didn't fly here from Syracuse to see only you!"

It was Debbie! Of course, it was Debbie. Plastic Santa had missed Debbie; she was always the voice of reason. She spoke with the kind cadence of her mother.

"I was going to repaint his coat and his belt before we put him back outside. The kids have been hounding me to get it done. I haven't had a moment since we moved in. Dad brought it up to me when we were at the veteran's home this past Sunday."

"Don't you dare paint him! How could you do that?" Debbie's voice was soothing even when she was angry.

Daniel laughed. "Okay, okay. Let's get the kids settled in for tonight. Tomorrow, after breakfast, we can put him out on the porch. I will let *you* plug in his light."

"Yes, you will," she said with fervor.

Peering over the chipped and faded balusters surrounding the loose floorboards of a Victorian sitting porch stands a forty-six-inch-high plastic Santa Claus.

This Saint Nick was picked up on a whim during a late-fall shopping trip to Sears and Roebuck in 1968. His bright blue eyes had seen plenty of cheer, and some sadness, from his holiday season vantage point overlooking the corner of Lincoln Street and Farrington Avenue.

His now re-energized internal sixty-watt bulb cast a warm glow across the lawn and to the frost-cracked sidewalk beyond.

Daniel mentioned to the family that the lightbulb was "Brandy-new."

Late-Night Musical Musings

The General Electric table radio was tuned to Canadian broadcasts, and the crickets were working overtime as darkness overwhelmed the dacha in the woods of Washington County.

"It's gonna take a lotta love" trailed off as it was overwhelmed by the clarity of the breeze coming in from the Atlantic.

"Nope, that's Nicollette Larson. Trust me on this one."

"Are you sure? I'm thinking it sounds like Crystal Gayle," said Sammy.

I responded after a sip of black coffee. It took me a second, as I needed to chew a couple of coffee grounds that had skipped the filtering process.

"The reason I know this—willing to be open-minded in the '70s—is that I told some buddies that I liked this song; they questioned my masculinity. I didn't care, love the song. End of story. She passed in the late '90s. I was a bit sad."

And with that, we sat on the dark porch—I, in the open doorway overlooking the lake, and Sammy across the pine floor, sitting in a plastic chair whilst icing his swollen Achilles tendon.

My butt was inside on the stoop, but my legs and feet were a bit further outside, resting on the treads of the stairway. There are no mosquitoes to be battled in late summer, and an open door made the porch seem much more expansive.

Ellie sat by Sammy because he is her best friend outside her immediate family. She loves me, but she adores Sammy; he takes her outside every time she cries to go. He always complies. I don't because I know her game. She is good. I give her credit for never giving up.

Autumn was slipping in at an alarming pace. I could feel the difference on my face and bare feet, as my toes rubbed the residual moisture off the stair treads leading down to the overgrown lawn. I mused that I must mow that tomorrow.

I don't know what song followed that one; it wasn't familiar, but I had redirected the focus of my attention to the urgent call of one loon—maybe two—who seemed upset at something on the other end of the cove.

Autumn was coming to the jagged edge whether we invited her in or not. I'd embrace the change.

LATHER, RINSE, REPEAT. BUT NOT ON THE CAT

WITH AUTUMN FADING IN MY REARVIEW MIRROR, I REPACKED my travel bags for whatever came next. While my travels are typically confined within the borders of Maine, there are a few nuances between summer dunnage and autumn gear bags. I'd made the switch.

To the kid's house, I drive about 130 miles. To the camp? A bit over a buck. I normally sleep over at one of those two stops. It's good to carry a few things—to be prepared—in a state known for striking changes in weather.

I carry two bags when going away for an overnight—one big and one small. Both have someone else's initials embroidered on the side.

Yup, they came from the return racks at one of several L.L.Bean outlet stores. The bags are both the same shade of green, waterproof, with a zippered top. They are not suitcases, just tote bags. You can save a lot of money buying good stuff that someone else—with a different name—found didn't fit their fancy. Those screwed-up initials make it even cheaper.

Spare jeans, a couple of shirts—both tee and flannel—foundational garments (I picked up that phrase from 1960s Sears catalogs), fleece or sweatshirts, and an outer shell just in case.

The small bag carries flashlights, knives, multitool, chargers, a portable Bluetooth speaker, a computer, identification, and a few things that need to be toted because of my line of work. The dunnage bag can be thrown anywhere in the bed of the truck. The small one stays inside the cab for obvious reasons.

You probably wonder where the shaving kit was. So did I. I have all the stuff I need for hygiene breaks at the camp. What I don't carry is soap or shampoo. I figure if I slide into someone else's rain locker, there will be something to use for scrubbing. And I'd be right if my daughter-in-love wasn't such a spiffy housekeeper. The spare bathroom—typically used for baby baths—had a few toys on the edge of the tub. However, the shining shower was barren when it came to cleaning supplies for larger humans.

I had already started the shower and was in a dire state of undress when I realized there was no soap, shampoo, or something that would suffice for same. I exited the shower and began to dig, and drip, around the vanity and cupboards below.

Deep under the sink, I saw a bottle of Espree Tea Tree and Aloe. I grabbed it and slipped back into the shower with nary a concern that there was a photo of a basset hound wearing a cold compress decorating the bottle. I didn't notice the dog—at all—until well underway in the scrubbing process.

It really didn't matter; the soothing tea and aloe took away all my concern about using dog shampoo. I did make sure to check the bottle for other warnings, but I waited until after rinsing and repeating. I noted that the directions only specified that the shampoo was not to be used on cats. It made no mention of me.

When I later explained to the family that I utilized some soap from under the sink, I did take some ribbing. But it's tough to embarrass a guy who carries discount luggage emblazoned with someone else's initials. After all, what's good for the basset is good for the dander.

It should be noted that I have had zero concerns about dry skin or fleas since last weekend.

I digress.

LAWNMOWING LESSONS

MY KNOWLEDGE OF COILS AND SPARK PLUGS STARTED WHEN my cousin Ray asked me to hold the plug wire connected to a pull-start mower. I was rarely at Ray's house, but I was a trusting soul; I felt that he had only my best interest in mind. I held the wire; Ray pulled the rope. It hurt. I learned.

I became part of the rope-pulling hit squad as we duped other neighborhood kids into holding the wire. Soon, we ran out of victims, and we moved on to other pursuits, none of which included using the mower for its intended purpose.

Before Google and the Interweb, many lessons were quickly learned because of the pain that accompanied them. Little did I know that Ray saved me another painful lesson. His demonstration allowed me to avoid falling for the old "pee on the electric fence trick" a bit later in my life. With every negative comes a positive.

The lessons I learned about spark were deviously translated into a way to avoid the mundane task of mowing my lawn. It was the summer of 1973 and I was nine.

It was June, and I wanted to go brook trout fishing. Dad had gone to work and asked that I mow the grass. All I could think about were brook trout . . . and Tina. I don't remember her last name, but I suspect it has changed at least once by now, so it wouldn't matter anyway. Tina had shared with me that there was a stream where we could catch some trout. I wanted to go fishing, but for some reason, deep within my soul, I really wanted to go with Tina.

I devised a plan in which I would disconnect the spark plug wire some distance from the porch where I knew my mother would make her appearance. The tall grass and correct angle would keep the deviously disconnected wire a secret between myself and the Hereford bull that lived in the adjacent pasture. He was always staring at me, and he seemed trustworthy.

I also knew that Pete would be gone later in the fall, and he surely would not tell anyone after being wrapped in freezer paper.

Edith Carol is my mother, not a woman inclined to care much about mechanical things. My rudimentary knowledge of "suck, bang, blow"—the basics behind all internal combustion engines—was just enough to show her that when the lawnmower had no bang, I could blow off mowing the lawn. The job that sucked could be delayed until later in the week.

I began to methodically pull the starter rope while my mother watched out the window. I presented my "frustrated-face" knowing full well that I needed to make the sale to E. Carol. She was no fool, but my knowledge was power or lack thereof. If I played my cards right, I wouldn't need to tell her a lie. I could create a one-act play that allowed me to sell my story.

I was no Thornton Wilder, but I could present my short play about a lawnmower that wouldn't start. Very few lines were needed. The fewer the better—E. Carol could smell a lie when told by her children. All I could smell was raw gasoline as the little lawnmower that couldn't, didn't.

I said things like "Must be flooded," and "Maybe it will start later," to build a case for making my way down the Upper Ridge Road to a cool running brook that Tina had pointed out on our way home from school.

Excessive rope pulling turned to full-fledged flailing, and after several loud sighs were directed toward the screen door, Edith Carol entered porch right.

I let the rope snap back and the black rubber T-handle smacked the recoil cover in a satisfying bang. I stood up straight and said, "It won't start." I had not lied. Edith Carol asked me why; I said, "I will try it again later."

I should have continued showing a frustrated face, or shrugged more, but she bought it. She walked back into the house, unimpressed but also unconcerned. I went fishing with Tina.

Tina and I only went fishing together on that one occasion. I had no idea—in that passionless moment—why trout fishing with a girl was so much fun. We caught nothing. Tina never called me again. Shocking, I know. I think she liked me for my collection of nightcrawlers. I hope she has since recovered from the devastating loss.

My scheme worked well on a couple more occasions during that summer. I employed the trickery and deceit when Laura—from Cape Elizabeth—came to visit her aunt at an old farmhouse about a mile up the road.

Laura had braids, and, fortunately, she also had a brother. I say "fortunately" because I needed her brother to be the shill in my scheme to hang out with Laura. I don't recall his name. It didn't matter. If I was going to create an illusion to Edith Carol that the lawnmower didn't start, I had no problem hanging out in a barn with Laura's brother while I waited for her to come out and get to know the man who had avoided mowing, yet again.

Showing up on the Western Flyer-branded stingray bicycle (incidentally coming from the same Western Auto where the intentionally nonoperational Wizard mower had been purchased) was definitely the way to make an entrance. Putting the kickstand down while still in motion was only one of the many moves that I believed would lead Laura and me to a life filled with love and whatever else came with it. I really had no idea how the relationship would progress.

Hopefully, if we both worked, we could pay someone else to mow our lawn.

Thick and sturdy hemp rope and an old hand-hewn wooden seat was the vehicle that would allow me to display my airborne skills of derring-do. She paid no attention to my masterful barn beam swinging. But she was just lovely. I went to visit the brother, but I stayed for the braids. I never saw her again either.

It should be noted that I always ended up mowing the lawn. I don't recall being asked about why on one day it would run and on another day it would refuse to start. Maybe my parents knew what I was up to, but I don't think so. If they had found out, I believe my intentional and preplanned procrastination would have sooner or later led to a plethora of punishment and perdition in perpetuity.

The takeaway? A rudimentary knowledge of the internal combustion engine can be an asset when trying to meet your future significant other.

You can employ any method you want to meet that special someone, but whether there is a spark, or not, sooner or later you will still have to mow the lawn.

(Originally published on *CarTalk.com*)

LEFT TO OUR OWN ADVICES

THE PICKUP TRUCK WAS WALLOWING ABOUT ON MY LAST journey to the east coast. While it is heavily sprung, and the roads are bad from here to eternity, I felt that the steering inputs caused it to be a tad more squirrelly than typical.

I had a heavy trailer in tow, and that certainly exacerbates any asphalt-derived irregularities. I chalked it up to improper tongue weight and incorrectly inflated tires.

I wouldn't say I am a stickler for maintenance, but I pay attention and keep up with the necessities. I enjoy the feeling that I get when the oil has been freshly changed and the tires rotated to opposite sides and opposite ends. It seems that engines feel like they run smoother and quieter after new oil has found its way to the crankshaft and all the other internal bearing surfaces.

I think it's a psychological smoothness, merely a self-imposed moment of motorized Zen. Still, it's good to know there are five thousand more miles between you and the next belly-crawl under the filthy chassis.

As I was killing a bit of time between destinations, I manipulated the steering wheel-mounted controls so that the tire pressures would be shown on the dash screen right before my very eyes. It's the one feature that I think should be standard equipment in all new vehicles. I don't trust that the numbers are 100 percent accurate, but it's a good starting point when next you find yourself handy to an air hose. Seeing the pressure in digital form is much more informative than getting a flashing yellow light on the dashboard that looks like a tiny flat tire.

I noted that the right-front tire was about five pounds below the manufacturer's recommended pressure, and the two back tires were also severely lacking in the inflation department. (I would have written that they were slacking, but that's too easy and could be considered grammatically inferior wordplay.)

I made a mental note that I would take a few minutes—when I returned to Bangor—to check them with a proper air pressure gauge. I usually have a compressor with me on working weekends, but this time I'd left it behind, knowing that there would be no need for it; I was wrong again.

My Sunday morning coffee, church, more coffee, car wash, pastry run, newspaper-reading on the waterfront, bagel-munching session allowed me some time for tire pressure checks. I dug into the back-door cubby to dig out the old electronic gauge. It's a nifty device that displays the pressure numbers with glorious LED clarity.

I could see on the tiny screen that the battery was low, but I believed it could still be trusted to give me a few checks before going to the dark side for good. I would change the battery later.

I added the appropriate amount of air to each of the ten-ply tires. It seemed to take forever, and it made my knees ache because of the time spent in the kneeling position. I should do more of that for other reasons, but the tarmac made it a painful endeavor. I prayed for sweet relief, as well as a more powerful compressor the next time I took on the task.

My target goal was sixty pounds of pressure in each of the front tires and sixty-five pounds in the rear tires. Still, it took far longer to reach the needed threshold than I expected. I stuck with it. I used my electronic gauge between each dose of air, and while the device seemed to be a bit wonky, I reached my goal on each of the Kevlar-reinforced Goodyears. I've put a lot of air in tires and never had it seemed to take so long to add enough to get the required pressure readings.

I kicked the last tire like a seasoned specialist, and I surmised that the pressures were—now—certainly higher.

My first few miles were jolting to the capped cup of coffee in the center console. Black bean-juice shot forth like lava from Vesuvius out of the singular sipping slot. This Goodyear-related geyser was not normal behavior for my cups of coffee, even on Maine roads. Our frost-blasted byways should not be confused with your "Main" roads. The additional "E" denotes the fact that we have *extra* potholes.

The jolting was jarring, and I am an affirmative fan of a firm ride. Passing a couple of cars on the northbound I-95 turned into a full-fledged hellish sleigh ride, and I slowed to below the posted speed limit to inquire what the heck was going on. Upon my quivering manipulation of the steering wheel controls, I discovered why it took so long to fill the tires with air.

Each of the displayed digits indicated approximately ten more pounds of pressure than required by the manufacturer's suggestions provided to me on the door-jamb sticker. While I could easily explain away a pound—or two—in either direction of being exactly spot-on, these numbers were far higher than those that had been displayed on the faded screen of my tired tire gauge.

I concluded that the pain in my knees had been brought on by a weakened battery in my electronic air-pressure checker. I spent about double the time in the crouching-tiger position than I should have. This also shed some light on why the wall-mounted gas station air dispenser strained so much while filling up my tires. I had been pushing Zeppelin-level air pressure into a tire meant to be filled with far less.

No, I can't explain how the gauge could have been recalibrated by a weakened battery to read ten pounds too low in the pressure category, but I did glean a life lesson from the Conestoga-like ride quality that was my gift after trusting the badly behaved device.

In life, we sometimes depend on the wrong people for good advice. Yup, I should have double-checked the pressures on the dash-mounted device soon after topping off the tires. Relying on one gauge—or one person—for the best advice is not always the correct course of action.

Additionally, I depended on that one device while disregarding the low-battery warning and wonky behavior. Yet, I still accepted its information as "pure gospel." I should have known better. I do now. I have added a new air pressure gauge to my gear, and it doesn't rely on battery power.

Nope, this story really isn't a devotional, but my knees still ache, probably for the wrong reasons.

Surround yourself with wise counselors, check their batteries (or background) before depending on their advice. In a society where we receive much commentary and unrequested input from SMO (social media only) friends, we need to exercise caution.

Getting bad advice can make many things—even tires—much harder.

LINT

IT HAD BEEN ABOUT A WEEK SINCE I'D DONE A LOAD OF laundry; the white, flimsy plastic basket with a missing handle held the standard fare.

I can get by doing one to two loads a week. There were two pairs of jeans, an appropriate number of undergarments, socks, various plaid shirts that look very much alike unless you are a connoisseur and can appreciate the subtle differences between a Carhartt and a slightly pilled long-sleeved flannel from L.L. Bean.

On top of the pile, teetering in preparation for a fall, was one pair of uniform pants with a mayonnaise stain just above the right knee. That stain was a testament to a delicious, canned-chicken sandwich that got away from me on the upswing from plate to mouth.

The chunk of chicken hit me with a vengeance, and it marked its spot like a muddy-footed mixed-breed retriever might leave a print on an ornamental Oriental rug as he returns from a nonsanctioned spring romp in the swamp. I hit the spot hard with cold water and a paper towel to keep the stain from setting.

Dark blue uniforms hide stains, but they also keep secrets that are only dragged out by a thorough cleaning.

I blasted the spot with Shout, launched the entire pile into the front-loader, and switched the timer to a thirty-minute cycle, as I thought fifty-five minutes would be overkill. I knew twenty-five wouldn't quite cut the mustard, or, in this case, the mayonnaise.

The washing machine cycled through its everyday noises while I read a little and mindlessly scratched the dog's ear while she snored—intermittently—as the pressure of her head put my right leg to sleep.

The tingling became bothersome, but I didn't have the heart to move her away from her spot. She spends lots of time alone these days. When she gets a chance to sleep against a human, she seems to engage in deep slumber. I felt obliged to let her stay right there. Rubbing a dog's ear directly in the warm and fluffy spot where the ear attaches to the head is therapeutic in a way, and not just for the dog. If you have a dog, you know exactly what I am speaking of.

After the spin cycle became a still and static pile of damp duds, I prepared the dryer's lint screen by removing remnants of washes past.

Dark blue lint, mixed with various shades of unidentifiable cloth fiber, made up most of the matted mess of material. As I thoughtlessly tossed the dark blue ball of fuzz into the trash can, I saw several former lint-screen leavings sitting in the bottom of the can. Much of it was dark blue; much of it had been shed during multiple cleanings of the same uniforms.

I am not a man who considers himself worthy of writing parables. It seems pointless to attempt to put into words all the thoughts that run through my head in an ordinary day. Most of these thoughts wouldn't make sense to another human, just as their thoughts wouldn't make much sense to me.

I don't expect visions, deep voices, or writings scrawled on a wall by unseen hands. I don't throw lint in a trash can expecting it to be a spiritual event. But the lint was representative of what is left behind, every day, by every cop in America.

It can easily go unnoticed, for it is pulled away incrementally and over long periods. We don the uniform again and again. It becomes soiled with the sights, sounds, words, tears, and deeds of the person wearing it, but it also collects the same from those who encounter it.

I turned off the light and walked away from the dark blue lint as the dryer toiled away, adding a little more to the recently cleaned screen.

The dog hadn't moved from her spot on the couch, and my fingertips found the soft area just behind her ear. It's therapeutic, but not just for the dog.

Magnetic North on Eisenhower's Highway

Magnetic north pulled me up the black macadam toward a tiny Cotton family reunion. It would be one of us heading up, two of us heading back.

While the distance is a curse, the drive is not. I-95 beyond Bangor, Maine, sauntering toward Canada, is a lonely stretch of road. Most of the cursing on this odd-numbered Maine-to-Florida Interstate is more prevalent below D.C. and through the Carolinas. On this ribbon of Eisenhower's masterpiece, any cursing is futile. No one will hear you. That's what makes it one of my favorite drives.

I don't believe the mercury had found its way past zero when I picked up a black coffee in a paper cup. My vaporous breath met that of my baristas in the chasm between car and frosty sliding glass window. She shut it quickly, leaving my breath to have the last dance all by itself. I took the first sip with a bit of trepidation. I always worry that someone will add cream, forcing me to drive around the building one more time to correct the problem.

A north wind was redistributing the recent snow, removing it from the fir trees lining the highway. Balsam and spruce branches exhibit patience as they hold mother nature's manna. Depending on the prevailing winds, or a bit of sun, they wait to dump their cargo so that they can spring back up and play catcher for the next snowstorm.

On my northward and southward drive, I witnessed the process. The drama unfolding all around me created a smoke-like mist of snow swirling through the air. Indeed, I would have relished being somewhere a bit further into the woods to watch the show. Still, the beauty is more difficult to embrace when the itinerant snow showers force the frozen precipitation down your collar and into your face.

Honestly, if it weren't for the road through all of this, I would rarely witness the spectacle.

I pointed out the snowy tornados to my tiny passenger on the way home. She listened for a time, but she was more interested in a short nap. I turned the radio down to a level commensurate with her tolerance for noise and cracked my window so that I could feel a few of the speeding flakes melt upon my face.

I believe that someday she will enjoy these long drives as much as I do. For now, I'll appreciate the cold snow on my face and the warm feeling in my heart.

Many Moons Ago

THE CRESCENT MOON SETTLED INTO THE TOP—FAR LEFT—pane of the twelve available to me in the bedroom window. Due to the angle of my head—laying on the pillow—the moon was the center of attention when I opened my eyes.

I didn't look at my watch, but only because I didn't need to. It was 3:00, give or take five minutes.

On my favorites list, the waning crescent moon is second only to the full moon phase. I stared for a few minutes in a quest to take it in before I might be able to doze off again. Staying in bed until 4:00 a.m. was my goal. I didn't make it.

The moon moves to the east, but the earth turns in the same direction. It makes for some interesting viewing angles. I was happy to be part of it for a couple of minutes. How many waning crescents have I missed by being silly while I waited for the sun to come up to slither out of bed?

It's been a long time since I regularly worked midnight shifts. I started my police journey in a smaller town than Bangor. The cops there worked out their run of midnight shifts alone, six or seven in a row.

Shortly after 2:00 a.m. each night, the sergeant and one other patrol officer would get off shift, and you would be left as the last man standing.

On the slow nights, and there were a bunch, you could pull down to the marina on the Penobscot River, get out for a stretch, and lean on the warm hood of your Chevy whilst sipping a hot coffee.

You could pick up a cup from Dunkin Donuts over on Odlin Road. You had to drive across the town line into Bangor if you wanted to buy a coffee after 3:00 a.m. It was on a regular route of travel from one road to another, so there were no issues with leaving the confines of suburban America; it was for coffee, after all.

Once strategically parked and overlooking the wide river, it was essential to turn up the center-mounted Motorola radio. Then, you had to click on the portable radio riding on your hip so that you would be sure not to miss a call when you were out of the car for a few minutes.

It was also imperative to turn up the mono speaker of the AM/FM radio to the Phil Hendrie Show. Blending the two audio feeds was an art. You had to be able to listen to Phil's insane "guests" but also be able to hear Linda or Debbie from Dispatch.

They often needed to send you somewhere to help somebody who was also not sleeping, usually for different reasons— most of them, terrible.

The morning's waning crescent looked like many I have gazed upon before. Some nights, I would be snickering in the dark while listening to Phil and sipping a medium with two and two. I gave up cream and sugar about six years after becoming a cop. Black coffee was easier to order.

You, alone, are responsible for the taste of your coffee when you order black. It's good to have that kind of power and authority. You really don't have control over many other things on a midnight shift as a cop. Black coffee and the reliability of the moon phases were two things you could always count on.

Well, that, and the laughs provided by Phil Hendrie.

NEVER MOVE A PIANO ALONE

THE MAN WAS TRYING TO STRAP DOWN THE OLD PIANO ON A trailer—on a hill, in the rain.

I didn't stop to help him. That sums up my haunting regret for the weekend.

The whole scene happened quickly, and I was hauling a tractor on a trailer—going up the hill, in the rain—when I passed him. I kept on going.

Stopping would have been far more dangerous for the traffic that followed me. After years of watching people with good intentions pull over in unsafe spots, creating hazards for others, my left arm won the battle against the right, and I didn't stop.

The thing is, I've been there, and I needed a hand. Now and again, people have stopped. Micro-friendships have been nurtured in those few minutes of shared commiseration over poorly tied-down cargo. I missed out on the chance to say to him, "I feel your pain."

I also channeled his feeling of embarrassment. It's a familiar and powerful feeling when you become a focal point of failure, sitting on the side of the road, inquisitively holding cargo straps. At the same time, you consider your dilemma viewed by people who pass on their way to more pleasant events. I felt that too.

Still, I rolled on, straining to peer back in my rearview to see if someone else—without six-thousand pounds of baggage— would stop to help. Maybe someone in a Mazda. A Mazda could be tucked onto the shoulder just beyond that poor guy's upright and poorly tuned Waterloo.

I've moved pianos but never alone. I considered that as I drove to my destination. I then began to feel sad that the man was alone. But I've been there too.

If there was a T-shirt slogan that comes out of my morning of shared and regretful misery, it would say, "Never move a piano alone."

I must believe he figured it out—not only how to secure that old thing on his trailer, but that he finally got some help to install the crusty, upright church piano into his chosen setting.

I hope that within a few weeks, some kid will be taking piano lessons on that piano. People will become more regretful that it was moved there in the first place.

Later, when the kid excels at math, plays for a crowd at church, or for the family on Thanksgiving, all that roadside embarrassment will ride away on the notes created by the tiny, felt hammers that refuse to rest inside their cabinet.

When his child moves out, he can help someone load up the big, brown behemoth and send it to another home. Pianos are like transient ghosts. They just keep haunting new homes after being moved up hills. On trailers. In the rain.

Never move a piano alone. Better yet, don't let your friends move pianos alone. We all should know better.

Ninety-One Minutes, Forever

Driving in twilight eliminates unnecessary distractions. Said to be the most dangerous time on the road for a driver, our eyes naturally readjust to ready for the darkness that follows—too soon.

Shadows develop into imaginary features and creatures. Branches become arms, reflectors become eyes, and our imaginations are left to sort out the details.

Distant roadside landmarks are no longer available for us to use for comparison, and our world becomes a little bit smaller. It's a good time for introspection.

Twilight is longer in the summer than in the winter. During June, it lasts about ninety-one minutes. It officially begins at sunset and ends when that same sun tucks itself six degrees below the horizon. I've no way to gauge that. My hope is to drive fast enough, far enough, to make twilight last just a bit longer than the scientific explanation allows.

Twilight became my focus last week. I can't say when it moved to the forefront of my mind. I believe it happened within a ninety-one-minute window of time during a musically choreographed drive to the woods of my beloved Washington County.

When the light of a retreating day is angled—just right—I can feel it. I've never discussed this with anyone, but only because I have difficulty explaining it. Does that feeling wash over me because of the uncontestable happiness of surviving

another day, or because of my pleasure in seeing the twinkling—flickering—hope from the retreating light as it strug-
gles through the gaps in the surrounding canopy of dark green?
I'm not sure.

Fifteen years ago suddenly seemed closer than the sweeping
curves of the asphalt trail that slices a few minutes off the trip
between Ellsworth and Cherryfield. I had placed the paper
coffee cup to my lips when I heard some shuffling from the
backseat. I knew it was Ellie readjusting in her tight quarters,
but the darkness filling the truck allowed it to morph into the
sounds made by a nine- or ten-year-old boy who made the trip
with me hundreds of times. He couldn't be shoehorned into
that space now, but he fit quite perfectly for about twenty years
of these twilight jaunts.

I waited for a scratchy-voiced question, but it didn't come. I
strained to hear the voice, but only darkness resonated through
the cab of the truck.

I listened for a while. I finally turned with a squinting hope
that I'd see him with his head leaning into a crumpled, window-
propped, sweatshirt as he slept—peacefully—despite the wash-
board roads. Having a passenger who trusts you enough to fall
fast asleep is a silent compliment to the security that you have
provided to them. Trust from your child is one of the rewards
that fills the empty shelves inside the partitioned soul of a
parent.

I saw a ball of fur curled tightly against the camp dunnage
and my red metal toolbox. She didn't hear the voice either. I
refocused on the road and attempted to recall some of his questions that I'd answered multiple times. Tonight, I could have

answered all of them succinctly and correctly. I couldn't have done that fifteen years ago.

Time and distance have a way of making all our answers a perfect explanation. These perfect answers are only made possible as the passage of time mutes all your mistakes, and it even tempers a few responses that I now regret.

Officially, twilight only lasts ninety-one minutes in the middle of June. But if you free your mind to wander, it can last forever.

Observations from the Ride to Work

When attempting to re-home old upholstered furni-ture, it's understood that many Mainers appreciate the roadside display of free offerings.

Furniture shopping from the seat of a slow-moving Chevy Silverado—with rusty, yet still state-inspectable cab corners—does have its benefits in the time of a pandemic. Why mask-up to enter the clean and well-lit emporiums of similar furniture that is merely newer and odor-free?

Taking an opportunity to drive around your town—and several others—gives you a chance at finding some slightly more worn-out, torn, and completely soaked furniture right at the roadside, and ready for pickup.

There is no question that there is a buttock for every sofa, loveseat, or velveteen armchair—even when tattered to the point that it appears wolverines have been consummating in-appropriate woodland relationships within the foamy core.

One way to extend the life of a well-used-furniture lawn display is to remove the tattered blue tarp from the woodpile and place it over the outdoor collection of your formerly indoor furniture. The rain really has a way of making your "free for the taking" turn into a long-standing, moldy, roadside attraction.

A husband-and-wife team riding in the FTTGB (First Truck That Goes By) will often lock up the brakes and then gather up your formerly glorious living room set. However, there are times when it might sit for a few days.

People will notice when the Sharpie-inscribed makeshift cardboard signs have obvious runs and smears that make the double letter "E" (in "Free") appear to have been turned into—really elongated—number eights. This is but a tiny indicator that the furniture has endured one or two late-afternoon Maine summer deluges.

The lack of proper coverage of your treasures can slow the process of returning your lawn to a place for quiet reflection.

Be a responsible display(er) of used furniture.

ONCE UPON AN ON-RAMP

I PUSHED DOWN THE BLINKER LEVER AND TAPPED MY TOE onto the well-worn brake pedal. The feedback caused me to consider that I was braking a bit too late, but I would safely make it through the turn regardless of the thick slush that coated the frost-cracked tar.

I had an appointment about twenty-five miles south of my hometown. Interstate 95 is the conduit to greener pastures—at least, on this particular day.

I have been driving on ice, slush, snow, and—now and then—dry pavement for over forty years.

I turned the wheel a bit harder to the left and transitioned my right foot back to the throttle to give the front wheels the nudge they needed to pull me out of my easily controllable skid. It's not the skidding that gets you into trouble; it's the panic that sometimes accompanies a loss of friction between rubber and macadam.

If you have driven long enough in the snow belt of America, a skid is merely another opportunity to become a champion, a savior of steel and glass while utilizing only the skills learned from other—previous—skids.

The human brain is a magnificent time, speed, and distance calculator. The collection of the feedback and data was immediate, and without any conscious thought on my part. I believe that fleeting recollections of close calls from road trips past were retrieved with nary a millisecond to spare. That data directed my twin palms to apply the perfect amount of left-hand pressure, while my right foot received a dose of proper pedal modulative capability.

I missed the ice-covered guardrail by a meter or more, and I barely scuffed the stacked snowbank with the sun-faded right side bumper cover.

At about mid-skid, I was able to glance toward the hot coffee daintily dancing in the dash-mounted, retractable drink-holder. The cup appeared to be making independent plans to free itself. This was—most likely—caused by the cup's overwhelming fear of being entrapped during the impending crushing crescendo of man, machine, and mad multifunctioning musculoskeletal maneuvering.

In the end, not a drop spilled out of the adult-style sippy-cup cover that is currently all the rage among the caffeinated cowboys who ride the American highways.

Sure, there remained a standard dose of residual cold coffee that would ride within the rim of the cup's shallow gutter until spilled by an overzealous sipper. This miniature gutter is always topped-off by the drive-thru clerks who tend to high-five one another when they are able to install the ticking coffee time-bombs into the cars of drivers wearing white dress shirts and expensive ties. I was wearing no such thing—at least, not on that day.

So many of us ramble down these on-ramps every single day, and none of us considers where all the others are going. We look ahead to the long, dark ribbon of promises and possibilities, and we begin to contemplate when and where our next pass will take place.

I accelerated smoothly and began to consider the impending need to merge with all the others who had already had their own on-ramp revelations. It was doubtful that their left or right turn was as action-packed as mine. I turned up the radio hoping for the perfect blend of guitar and percussion, maybe some brass and woodwinds; was a dose of Earth, Wind & Fire a possibility?

You see, the algorithms and calculations continue as we dance our way to completely different destinations. We damn the other drivers who have the gall to get into the passing lane before we can manage to. We jockey for position, preplan passes, and make audible estimates about the closing speeds of those who are soon to become larger than life in our rearview mirrors.

Suddenly, the stalked becomes the stalker as we are quickly transitioned to the vehicle that is closer than it appears to be in that very same driver's rearview mirror. We curse the passer for violations of laws, all the while pressing our right foot down in order to keep up with them so that we can get the plate number in case we need to call them in for blatant and heinous traffic infractions.

The uncontrollable nuances of the road are the great equalizer. Purported progress slows us all down at some point as we catch up in the well-marked construction zones. We expound to our passengers that we are now directly behind "that jerk" who passed us about fifteen miles back. We all wonder what their hurry could have been, but we seem to forget our own.

I brought the green glider up to a speed that was fit for a straight shot down Eisenhower's answer to the need for smooth movement of people and their things. I've used this on-ramp hundreds of times. It's led me to meetings, vacations, funerals, and weddings. It's marked the beginning of arguments, makeup kisses, joyous reunions, and some very sad days.

I readjusted my grip on the wheel and reached for the now-settled cup of coffee. I brought it toward my lips and then stopped—suddenly—just short of the sipping zone. The capped container gave me a twelve-ounce tactile Ted Talk regarding Newton's First Law of Motion as the hot dark roast proved the scientist's revelations to be 100 percent correct yet again. The sloshing confirmed all of it.

I held the cup a bit higher in a vaguely waved toast to my run down the thousand-foot runway of time and pressure-hardened petroleum and aggregate. I had places to be. I turned up the radio to drown out the buffeting noise of the seventy-mile-an-hour wind through the ancient side-window seals; I found that Green River Ordinance was up to the task. "On Your Own" began to soulfully—and statically—narrate my journey perfectly.

With so many of us rambling down these ramps every day, we should spend some time considering where all the others are going. We should also take a bit of time to contemplate and determine our destinations. On-ramps are good interludes for these kinds of considerations.

I took a sip of coffee, spilling none of the remaining residual remnants from the recessed rim down the front of my winter jacket. Winning at sipping can still be considered winning. Why do we not celebrate more of these tiny victories of life?

ONE BAD APPLE

FLEETING THOUGHTS DON'T ALWAYS STICK AROUND LONG enough for me to jot them all down. As of late, I have much about the blooming spring—and the chores that come with it—on my mind.

There are undertakings at the camp that demand my attention. While I am not the primary carpenter working on the minor porch rejuvenation job, I have been charged with adding a few electrical outlets before the interior walls are covered with rough-cut pine. Success will depend on what happens the next time I turn on the circuit breaker.

I need to open the neighbor's cottage, haul and stack some lumber, install a couple of docks, meet the soil scientist to find out where the new septic field is going to be located, move a cord of dry wood (in hopes that it might be a better spot for a leach field than for wood storage), and reset the front steps. Mr. Frost came in and did what he does best—that is, to make formerly level things crooked again.

The one hundred miles between camp and home are constantly trampled upon during my comings and goings. It gets expensive to live so far away from my favorite piece of ground. You learn to economize on other things, but the time to complete the tasks is allotted to each one of us in the very same way; there is never enough. I'll make the trip a total of three times this week, and I will not spend even one night sleeping out on the screened-in porch. The paying job back home takes precedence.

The good news is that I am catching up on some really great music and consuming various blends of convenience store coffee. I find myself quietly reviewing each offering while taking my first sip. "Mmm, it tastes like coffee," is clearly what this aficionado is hoping to mutter as he grabs the column shifter and drops the tranny into "D," for delicious, and then steers toward the "E" on the mirror's electronic compass. The "W" is used as a guide on the return trip. If not for the coffee, on some days, I might be reciting lefty loosey, righty tighty. That will do me no good when trying to get back home in the dark.

I smile to myself wondering what it would be like to drink a coffee that required me to utilize more than one descriptor—or even one extra ingredient—during the process of ordering. I've stood in a Starbucks line while the more refined in front of me rattled off the list of necessities that must be included in their bean juice. By the time I hear someone add the term "half-caff," I lose interest in the recipe. To be able to step up to the counter and say, "black," gives me a feeling that I might be giving the barista a break from the rote memorization exercises that terrorize them daily.

So far—this week—I have tried Honduran, Guatemalan, and Rwandan blends. All of them have been dispensed from those fancy instant brewing machines that grind out the beans after you used the digital screen to pick your poison. I really like the coffee that comes out of those things. I feel invested in the process. During brief discussion with the more outgoing clerks in various locations I have been informed that cleaning these fancy coffee makers is less time-consuming than the old type.

I embrace each poorly planned trip because destinations can sometimes be a letdown, especially when you cannot spend even one evening out of the three sitting by an open fire while being serenaded by peepers and the groaning of the lovelorn bullfrogs. That time will come, just not this week.

Ellie is confused with the repeated trips with very little downtime between the back and the forth. She would love to spend the night rather than winding down the hours snoozing in the backseat during the bumpy rides, but she makes it clear with her eyes that she will take the truck seat over the love seat every single time. She does take her mandatory swim upon our arrival. I avoid doing the same this time of year.

If I were a builder, I would never have been considered a good finish man. I'd be thought of as a rough carpenter, at best. Maybe I would be the guy they send out to get lunches and pick up materials at the lumberyard. I'd forget things, but I'd show up on time, and I would stay late if they needed me to. I'd rather be considered loyal and trustworthy than as the guy who does the work of a perfectionist. I would also guarantee that everyone got the fries they ordered, even if they were perched at the top of the bag. You need to be trustworthy with French fries, that's for sure.

It would be great to be skilled in the building trades; I would have saved piles of money over the past fifty years.

My writing skills are only about one step away from my carpentry skills. Some might say that is an egotistical over-statement. I can rough in a sentence, but I must come back more than once to grammatically improve the delivery and appearance.

I'm not complaining about my chores, my gas bill, my lack of quality writing skills, good planning, or being void of competency in carpentry. This is just more musing from the mind of a mope. Sometimes, it's the drive that gives me pleasure.

As I was writing this, Ellie came forth to express her need for sweet relief. While she was indisposed during the disposal of whatever was no longer necessary, I perused the arthritic branches of my old apple tree. It's a resilient soul.

I've been watching last year's sturdy and stubborn crab apples decaying away throughout the winter. I have wondered when the birds might pick the old fruit clean from the branches. Today, I was taken by the vivid pink flowering buds surrounding the remaining freeze-dried fruits from last winter.

It's difficult to pick out the carcass of the tiny apple, but the little rascal is hanging in there—sad, wrinkled, and brown—just about in the center of the frame. While no one would consider it a beautiful example of an apple—and it pales in comparison to the excited, vibrant, and youthful buds that surround it—it's still an asset to someone. Maybe a tired and northbound traveling bird will find it to be a nourishing tidbit. It could also be destined to drop to the ground where it will feed our tiny segmented and multilegged brethren who deserve some fiber too.

Some might label the fruit as an aging soul surrounded by young and beautiful individuals in much better condition. Another viewpoint to consider is that the apple could have made a conscious choice to linger longer to pass on some sage advice to those who are less experienced.

All of us have some value, no matter what stage of life we are in, even if we don't have the skills equal to those with whom we find it necessary to compare ourselves.

Even a rotten apple can help us come to a poignant ending in an essay about nothing in particular.

Oysters and Pot Roast

I could have written about the wind, but I have already done that. I'm not saying that I won't write about the wind on another occasion; it's just that this wind didn't seem friendly right then. It blew hard and cut through me while I stood outside and watched Ellie sniff the same spots over and over again.

I wore my mad bomber hat outside last night, and it's a good thing that I did. The dog took an inordinate amount of time assessing situations that no one else could see.

I was glad I wore the warmer, ear-flapped hat. It's similar to Randy Quaid's hat in the sewer scene in *National Lampoon's Christmas Vacation*. It's warm, and I was wearing pants, so this segment is not worthy of discussion.

I could have written about the leftover pot roast that I dug out of the fridge for last night's dinner. But that sentence merely made me wonder why the abbreviated—and acceptable—word for refrigerator adds the letter "d" in the center.

This makes no sense to me, and that's the kind of thing that happens in my mind when I open the door of the fridge.

My brother-in-law showed up with one thousand oysters. We discussed pricing as he was not bringing them specifically for me; he was selling them, and he already had a buyer. I could have purchased a few for dinner—I like all seafood—but still I opted to head to the fridge for more pot roast. He came—and left—with one thousand oysters in tow.

By the way, the carrots tasted divine. Their visitation with the potatoes and roast—for a couple of days in the fridge—was really good for them. Good company has a way of rubbing off on you.

I suspect my day was no different than yours, so it's not really worth writing about—or is it?

Why do we think our day needs to be exciting or remarkable to write about it or talk about it?

Instead, we scan the Interweb for an exciting video that had been shared by someone we didn't know. We find a meme that makes us smirk, and we share it. We look at others and determine that their day must have been more exciting. I can tell you that it probably wasn't.

People all around you are feeling the same way that you do. They burn their hand on the stove and reach into a cluttered cupboard to try to find the ointment that isn't there. They frantically rummage through drawers that are disheveled and ask cohabitants if someone might know where the cream is. Then, they run out to Walgreens to purchase a new tube of what they already have but cannot find.

Upon returning, the old ointment tube is miraculously discovered in another drawer. Economically, it makes sense to return the ointment that was just purchased, but, in the end, the new cream isn't returned at all. It's placed in the cupboard, and a mental note is made to try to use the old tube before opening the new one.

It'll be a couple years when this all plays out again, and guess what—that drawer will still be a mess. See, we are all remarkably the same. I find that comforting during times like these.

Some days you are offered oysters, but pot roast is just fine.

PAM

CRUNCH, CRUNCH, CRUNCH. CRYSTALLIZED COATINGS OF FROZEN precipitation called for caution. I scraped the windshield to create a porthole to the world ahead.

She had left the old Green Glider in the short-term lot and placed the keys in our secretly agreed-upon location. I only possess one set of keys. Regardless of admonishments and friendly warnings, I've not gone to the hardware store to make an extra set.

Usually, I take her to the airport. I couldn't do that today. A sleeping toddler with an appetite for Jimmy Dean sausage slept peacefully in the "Minnie Mouse Room." Not unlike the Lincoln Bedroom, it is a place of honor and only used on special occasions.

Late in the day, I hijacked my buddy Sammy to provide a ride to the airport to pick up my daily driver. It was covered in ice. Misty sleet had overpowered the warmer temperatures of a recently passed December. The ice settled nicely on anything that sat motionless for over an hour. I scraped the side window too. The old beast doesn't heat up for a time, and I do like to see as I drive.

Parking ain't cheap, and I thought I had arrived in time to save myself from the next tier of short-term terror; it's an hourly service.

The good news is that the kind lady in the warm booth understood my plight as I dug through my wallet for another five-dollar bill. She could see that our intention was a long-term spot, and I was merely a pawn being used for my prowess in pickup and skill with a scraper. A slight discount was applied. That set me free from the lift-gated prison of parking.

What a lovely woman. She had kind eyes and a smile that could only be better utilized by someone who makes you warm chocolate chip cookies when you come in from sledding on the hill at the park.

"Do you work here every day?"

"No, just on Sundays," she said.

"I come here a lot. How do you take your coffee . . . cream and sugar?"

She smiled. "You don't have to do that!"

"I don't *have* to do anything. That's the beauty of being me. Cream and sugar?"

"All of it," she smirked.

Pam fixed it. I believe that Pam fixes all kinds of things. I would see her again soon, and I wouldn't come empty-handed. My baking skills are not up to snuff, but I can buy a mean cup of coffee.

She even held me there just long enough for my windows to fully deice; I think it was in her plan the whole time.

Problematic people are working in a lot of public roles. We run into them, blood pressure rises, and tempers flare.

Then, you run into Pam. Suddenly, everything seems to be just fine.

Be the Pam.

PEEPERS

I DON'T FEEL THE NEED TO TELL PEOPLE WHEN I AM SAD. I'M not even sure I've ever met the threshold that certifies you as being officially sad or depressed. There are so many that I've spoken to who wanted to tell someone about it. I've listened, but not as well as I should have.

You think about that sometimes, depending on the day, the mood, or the spot in the sky where the sun has settled.

I've certainly been unhappy on more occasions than I care to think or write about here. Some of those stretches seemed endless, but end, they do. I visualize life in cyclical terms, and to be happy all the time would be a sad state of affairs for me.

The lows make highs better, but too many highs would bore me to tears. I've been around many people who seem happy all the time; I tend to be suspicious, but I remain hopeful for them all. I'm rooting for you, annoyingly delighted people; I'm rooting for you from the bottom of my heart.

Conversations between my old work partner and me concluded with a 2-0 consensus that we are far different people than we were in our younger years.

It's hard for us to admit that the job changed us. Within a few miles—and several dredged-up and orally supplied examples per person—while still clutching paper-cupped coffees that became cold from the lack of concern that we paid for them, we shake our heads in the affirmative that it's destroyed much of our serotonin regeneration.

We also cannot believe how fast it destroyed the happiness levels of some of our coworkers. Some of them left this trade without staying on long enough to be unhappy, or so we think.

"They've only been doing this job for three years! I can't believe they decided to quit and become a carpenter because of what they've seen! We've been doing it for over thirty years, and look how resilient we are."

Of course, we both know that we are not resilient at all. No longer genuinely pliable, silly things make us mad; sitting in traffic when we should be moving faster finds us verbally berating the drivers who can't hear us. Our significant ones have told us we've changed, but could it actually be them that have changed? How come the blame falls on us?

It has to be them. Right?

And so the narrative is typed up inside my head as I watch the dog sniff for far too long, searching for a place to pee under the golden glimmer of a quickly cooling evening lit by the remnants of a pretty darn good spring sunset.

"Come on, Ellie. You've literally sniffed all the same spots three times in the last five minutes."

The words came out with a lilt that sounded surprisingly kind compared to the frustration level I felt inside, probably because I'd just gotten a splinter in my foot from the deck that needs to be sanded and painted; I'll get to it.

Then came the peepers. From across the road, in a swamp that I've never set foot in, the peepers! I estimated there were at least ten, but I'm no peeper expert. I started to think about the winter they'd endured. These were the first peepers I'd heard this year—what a magnificent closure to a day that wasn't that bad. Imagine their pleasure when peeping proudly for the perfect mate to appear. I stretched and sucked in a full charge of cool air, and then I let Ellie sniff a few more spots.

I bet she loves the sound of the peepers too. I leaned over the rail and verbally urged her to sniff around for a few more minutes; who am I to call her inside?

Maybe we both just needed a dose of the spring peepers.

Play Ball

I DON'T FOLLOW PROFESSIONAL SPORTS WITH ANY REGULARITY. Indeed, I check the scores of Red Sox games, and I'll listen to about any baseball game on a transistor radio.

While America has needed baseball for many summers when despair was afoot, the past couple years have moved to the top of that list.

Yes, of course, you can still complain about salaries and the price of hot dogs, but at the same time, how many of us just *had* to have that fifty-inch television because the forty-seven inches just wasn't cutting it?

Sure, the commoner might be asking, "How big?" while a major leaguer might be asking, "How many?" but late-night baseball games broadcast over radio waves will do far more for us than therapists, alcohol, and pharmaceuticals.

Skip the new TV. It won't make a difference; dig out an old transistor radio this summer.

Comfortable and dulcet-toned conversations fill in the quiet spots between cricket outbursts and the annual mating growls from the bullfrogs who remain unseen on the shoreline of my favorite resting place.

Quiet voices in the background while reading a book eliminate the pleasant pangs of solitude that I seek with some regularity.

Baseball games—emitted from the radio speaker—remind me of riding with my dad in the 1965 Biscayne while I formed my outstretched right hand into the frontal shape of an air-plane wing when studying the flight dynamics of back road breezes.

For the sake of a warning, I also remember my left hand's flight dynamics going into a stall after being admonished by Mom.

"One young boy lost his hand by sticking it too far out the window when a tractor trailer drove by in the opposite direc-tion." I still think about that kid and sometimes wonder how he progressed through life without his left paw.

These thoughts only came to me when I began to read more about the stuttering start-up of the 2022 baseball season. I got a little worried for one of my close neighbors at the camp in the woods.

I cannot share his name or the details of his life, but the Red Sox game, broadcast from a leather-wrapped, nine-volt transistor radio, plays a considerable part of his one-week-a-year respite in the Maine woods. I cannot stand the thought of him missing out.

For that Fourth of July week, every summer of his fifty-plus years on earth, he eschews all things electrified and settles in to relive a bit of his boyhood. His radio—hung from a coat hook in the cabin—is tuned only to Red Sox games. He settles down on the porch at night, seated in a wobbly wooden chair while smoking. Thinking.

I can barely hear the radio, but I can see the glow of his Winstons flickering a bit brighter than the lightning bugs who flit about the heavy summer air. The resident nuisance box-a-dor, Ellie, finds her way over to push open his cabin's creaking back screen door. The snapping closure spring doesn't snap any-more. This leaves plenty of room for her nosy muzzle to swing the door open wide enough for the rest of her.

She checks his one-hundred-year-old kitchen for leavings and scraps and then exits through the front porch screen door when nothing can be found to snack on. Ellie sits with him for a few minutes, probably hoping for a nibble of something. I'll holler to her to "Get back over here," and he will yell back, "She's fine, Tim. She's always welcome over here."

That's as loud as we get in summer, just loud enough to communicate. We are not so loud that we break the calm created by the voices in the Fenway announcer's quarters or wherever the Sox might be playing that night. Ellie eventually returns, and my friend wanders back inside to find the empty chair where his father used to sit and listen to the games on the very same radio.

I only know these things because he told me. He shared— one afternoon—that when he comes for his silent week each summer, he sees his father sitting in that living room chair when the creaking back door swings open for the first time. Of course, his father isn't there.

That's why we need baseball back this summer—and every summer. It's not for me, but more for my summer neighbor. He needs to see his father. Especially this summer.

POACHED

WHO WRITES AN ESSAY ABOUT POACHED EGGS? NOT A MAN who is expecting others to take him seriously.

Oh, sure, there are serious bones in my body, but I keep much of that to myself. I choose not to become intertwined in deep conversations when someone expects me to interject some grand idea. My grand ideas are commonly downgraded to minor epiphanies once examined under the microscope of mob scrutiny.

Mob Scrutiny would be an excellent name for a band, wouldn't it?

I embrace simplicity, well-written directions, a straight line from A to B, a road with no curves, and yes, the song, *A Horse with No Name*. There is simplicity in riding a horse with no name, but only because such a horse could be referred to by any name that rolls off your tongue. The horse might not respond, so there is a downside.

I relish lyrics I can remember, famous quotes easily memorized, and I like my eggs poached.

Why would anyone waste their time writing an essay about poached eggs? Because no one has done it—at least none that I can find. I followed the straight line from the well-seasoned hand-me-down cast-iron frying pan to the stainless-steel poaching pot. My life is better for it. I only need to have my chief poaching pilot around the house to make my dream a reality.

Here is my dilemma: I have difficulty keeping the egg white and the egg yolk together during the boiling bath that creates the most impressive way to top off a piece of lightly buttered toast. I've listened to seasoned cooks explain how easy it is; I have done the homework; I have stared into the pot with my fingers crossed. I have good intentions, but the hen seeds do not often comply with my wishes.

The eggs become milky apparitions once they are cracked and dropped into the boiling water. They flit about the bubbling water in a way that makes fishing them out an exercise in futile fluidity. The yolks become independent loners who separate and stay away until they are herded onto a spoon and sadly slapped on top of the sourdough as an opaque orb of muted yellow putty; hard yokes in your poached eggs can never be considered a win.

The thing is, I do have a secret weapon, but she is only home for a few days at a time. Saturdays are the day of the planned breakfasts around here. On weekdays, I can only find time for coffee and something stale from a box. Sure, I sometimes settle for a couple of eggs—scrambled—after I liberate them from the cardboard carton that keeps them independently suspended and mutually exclusive. I would much rather have them poached.

One weekend past was like an alignment of the planets—shaped like eggs—because I have never before consumed any better poached eggs in my entire life.

When I mentioned that the eggs might have been the best that I ever ate, she explained the process while pointing out a few small details that I might have overlooked. I took notes.

She claims that the eggs are best poached when their internal temperature reflects the ambient temperature of the room where the poaching takes place; at our house, it's the kitchen. Such poultry-based sorcery was never explained to me before.

She shared with me that while she fries the bacon—always a nice touch—she allows the elected eggs to rest nearby to the open flame of the gas burner. It's as if they are relaxing and warming themselves by a campfire before heading over to the hot tub.

Her final secret—shared with me on a previous occasion—is that a person should always add a tablespoon of white vinegar into the boiling water before adding the nicely warmed eggs; this allows for fluffier whites. She believes that this step creates a better overall consistency in the final product.

Whatever she did, they were the best poached eggs I have ever consumed. She added fruit in the form of large blueberries and medium-sized grapes. I would have been fine with a few more slabs of bacon, but only because I am the one that must face down the dog, who never complains about the way the eggs are cooked. It's my fault, but I usually toss Ellie the last bite from each slice of bacon; she never misses, and when it comes to eggs, neither does the Missus.

When I groggily dropped her off at the airport on our spring-ahead day, I told her again that my best memory of her most recent visit was the poached eggs. She smiled and waved from behind her pile of wheeled luggage.

I went home and liberated a couple of eggs to the counter for some free-range time before directing them to the hot tub. You probably know how they turned out, simply because this essay is about *her* poached eggs. I still ate them, but I need a little more practice.

Potato Peeler

I don't want to come off to you as a guy who cooks a lot; the reason is, I never did—at least, until now. I have been trapped living a solitary life for the past few years.

This has led me to find several restaurants to take my money, and they have fed me in return for that money. I tend to order larger meals because I like leftovers, and I am also well-traveled in chubbier circles.

Pay no mind to the fat guy; he takes that pile of Styrofoam-stored chow home. Yeah, he might eat it on the way home, but he is hopeful that some will be left to take to work in the morning.

When my significant other stops by, she tears up the kitchen and prepares marvelous meals, but her visits were stopped for a time. She was getting many texts from me, mostly checking in and then asking her time and temperature questions regarding something I'd picked up at the local grocer. She's a good resource. When I cannot get a hold of her, I just go with 350 degrees until I see smoke; it has worked out fine.

But I must tell you that nothing gives me more pleasure than the utilization of simple tools—let me tell you about my vegetable peeler, because she's a dandy.

Sadly, your visit to my mind is brought to you by peeling vegetables for a soon-to-be horribly prepared roast beef dinner.

Sammy is coming over; he is a bachelor of the first order. Sammy will eat anything I cook. He never complains; he only demands that I do not prepare liver. For the record, I enjoy liver and onions. I used to order it at a joint on Broadway in Bangor. The waitress would tell me that I was the only guy who ordered it and that she thought it was "gross." I tipped her well as I like to talk to honest individuals.

While preparing potatoes and cutting the carrots for the day's epic dine-in, I began to contemplate the thought that went into the design of my satisfying and straightforward little buddy. It forced me to reach out to my sister, Google—she knows everything.

It seems that over five hundred versions of these little devils were patented in the 1800s. What a time to be alive—I mean if you lived past fifty.

Many attribute the invention to Thomas Williams, a blacksmith. If I were to be remembered for inventing something, the vegetable peeler seems like a grand way to be memorialized in an obituary. Anyone who reads the thing, or attends the service, could silently and solemnly give a gentle nod to the guy in the pine box who helped them obtain a substantial amount of nutrition throughout their lives. That's kind of a big deal.

Think of the time that was saved by Beetle Bailey. With the simple incorporation of some steel, bent in the shape of a "C," Beetle worked his way through multiple wars, many beatings by his sergeant, and he peeled tons of potatoes that fed all the members of his cartoon regiment.

It's something worthy of thought; isn't it?

Go ahead, watch your YouTubes, scan your Amazon accounts for a new series today. Read your books, stir your soup, and dig out the board games. The fact of the matter is that it is quite possible you wouldn't be alive—today—if Thomas Williams had just said, "Screw it," and continued putting shoes on horses.

Stay in, keep your paws clean, check on friends and shut-ins. Maybe something very cool will be invented this week, this month, or even this year. Boredom is the mother of invention.

PREENING DURING A PANDEMIC

MY BIRTHDAY—WHICH PUTS ME DEEP INTO AARP TERRI-
tory—was uneventful right up until 8:00 p.m. That's when I
determined that if I was going to cut my own hair for the first
time ever, it should be well after dark.

After watching about an hour of Wahl trimmer tutorial
videos on YouTube, I broke out the new clippers, and then I
got to work.

I have to say, I looked far less moronic than I thought I
would, and I would not be wearing a ball cap over the next
week, because I didn't even care.

When you are preening during a pandemic, people's expectations of perfection are not poignant.

I did find a baby picture that represents this hairstyle quite
well. My cowlick was epic. My sister in Chattanooga had recently shared it on my family page.

It was a good birthday. I FaceTimed with my lady-friend,
and I skipped supper; I was just too engrossed in blending from
a number two to a number four.

I wasn't leaving my barber, Dale. I never doubted that he
was making me look as wonderful as possible, but after this
hack-job, I missed him far more than I thought I would.

I learned from the whole pandemic that we need each other
more often than we thought we did.

As horrific as this whole mess is, when we come out on the
other side, we really should consider hugging a bunch of people
whom we never even thought about embracing before.

I won't hug my barber; I will just tip him better.

Recollections Created by Candy and Aftershave

I ENJOY GOING TO THE BARBERSHOP. I GO TO THE SAME BANGOR shop where my dad took me when I was twelve. Back then, the shop was owned by a pleasant man. He was a firm-handed gentleman named Ed Lingley.

Saturday morning at Ed Lingley's barbershop featured a blend of dads, sons, and a porridge of fragrances made up of Wrigley's Juicy Fruit gum, wintergreen mints, cigarette smoke, and Bay Rum aftershave. I still relish the odor created by three of those ingredients.

To a twelve-year-old boy, the smell of that shop was almost as intoxicating as a fleeting glimpse of some of the lithe ladies who hawked cigars, automobiles, and beer from between the worn pages of the sporting magazines strewn about the beat-up brown coffee table.

The table also held a couple of discombobulated newspapers that were separated by section. This satisfied the reading needs of multiple gents at the same time. As any recently read section was returned to the table, a newly seated customer would get an opportunity to partake in a slim segment of Saturday's news. The color comics might be left for the boys who were impatiently waiting their turn for a fresh high and tight.

The only hair out of place on Mr. Ed Lingley was an occasional clinger from one of his many customers; his own haircut was neat and tidy. It was combed over with just the right amount of grooming tonic. He wore a light blue nylon jacket that mimicked something more commonly worn by a dentist. I suppose the nylon was whisk-broomed off more easily. Peeking out from the top of that jacket was always a shirt and tie. His shoes were polished.

His image was one of a gentleman who served other gentlemen—classy, but with no judgment toward what his clientele wore during their visit. The weather was discussed regularly, but golf and fishing were usually up second or third.

In the latter years visiting the shop—after the throat cancer took Ed's voice—I recall that Mr. Lingley sometimes wore a pair of sneakers. I was in high school by then. He was probably seeking comfort after so many years on his feet.

He wielded electric clippers in one hand and his electrolarynx in the other. He never missed a beat when greeting folks who walked into the shop.

One or two second-string barbers worked alongside Mr. Lingley. They were equally skilled, but Ed was the quarterback. Many of the customers waited for a spot in his chair. They would wave off opportunities for a speedier haircut experience with another barber as they passed until Ed became available.

Even as a kid, I would feel sympathy for any new barber who did not have a full quiver of clients yet. I wondered if they felt slighted by the wave-off. While no one ever told me that I couldn't wave off a barber while I waited for Ed, it was clear to me that I was always to take the next open chair when my nod came. I knew my place in the pecking order of the inner sanctum.

During my high school years, when I drove down to Exchange Street on my own, I waited for Ed. I had already done my time in the minors. I attempted to add a vague apology for the wave-off by vocalizing, "Thank you, I'm waiting for Ed."

Still, to this day, I feel a bit of discomfort skipping the next open chair. In the decades since visiting Ed, I have learned that barbers understand that you need to feel at peace with the person who holds a razor to your neck.

I was in Lingley's old shop last weekend; he's been gone for years. The shop—essentially—has the same layout. It features newer equipment and multiple barbers and stylists. Most of my barbers have some connection to the original mothership that was Ed's shop. Some opened new shops in other towns, and some returned to the old building on Exchange Street when they realized the frustrations that come with running a one-man shop.

Building a loyal following cannot be easy. Some folks will bounce from barber to barber with no concern about who is cutting their hair. Some give the wave-off with nary a second thought to how it makes a new barber feel. Even a loyal core group of clientele cannot always follow their barber to new and exotic places. There is something comforting that lures you back to the place where you sat, one Saturday each month, over forty-five years ago.

The wait is different now; you must call ahead, and there is no more waiting inside and reading magazines. I ask for Dale. Over the last four decades, I have asked for George, Terri, Norm, Andee, a couple of Daves, and a fellow named Bob.

When the pandemic hit, I had to adapt—for a short time—to cutting my own hair. It was passable after several scary sessions, but I never did get the same results twice in a row.

I used multiple blade guards and dueling mirrors as I stood in front of the bathroom sink. I juggled, swapped the clippers from hand to hand, cut, shaved, and repeated the steps until it was far less than perfect.

What I discovered during this time was that my hair only needed to be cut short—Oh, and that YouTube videos were not going to take the place of a professional.

I was pleased when the shop reopened. Dale can trim around the ear strings on my mask with aplomb. We talk briefly about crime, but mostly about tractors, diesel engines, and future plans. Sometimes we talk about kids, wives, and grandkids.

Since masks became an everyday accoutrement, I began keeping wintergreen LifeSavers in the center console of my truck. I utilize them to make for a better personal experience when breathing in—and out—of a mask.

Recently, I discovered that the employment of these mints has the power to induce clear and concise recollections. LifeSavers—used at just the right time—can take you back in time.

Sure, it was Dale doing the cutting. But sometime between the hot towel and the neck shave, I could have sworn that I caught a whiff of 1976 sneaking into the room. Dale asked if I wanted any aftershave, and I told him the same thing that I always do.

"Bay Rum?"

Of course, he had it. They always have it.

I don't miss the smoke hanging in the air near the yellowing fluorescent lights, but I am considering picking up a pack of Wrigley's Juicy Fruit for my next trip back to the shop. I think Ed would approve.

RECYCLING THE POLITICIANS

IT SEEMS THAT I MADE THE NAUGHTY LIST AT THE POST OF-
fice. I should go in more than once a week.

My rented and locked metallic mailbox was empty except
for the yellow card that indicated I needed to see the principal
to pick up my weekly recycling. Looking behind the counter at
the blue-clad jugglers, I could tell they were not upset with me.
I believe they are probably sick of stuffing poster-sized fliers
into the tiny timeshare condominiums that hold postmarked
bills and letters from campaigning politicians.

I should make it known that I refuse to read cardboard
campaign materials, letters that address me as "Dear Sir," and
anything that feels like it's full of crap. I supposed it's just me
being a rookie curmudgeon.

I am also entirely sick of the notices being hung on my
doorknob at the house—mainly because when I enter the
abode, I find the throw rugs on the old hardwood floors are
several feet out of place.

No, the folks are not coming into the house and rearranging
the worn and poorly vacuumed foot-warmers, but Ellie is not
a fan of visitors to the porch. In her frothy attempts to bark
and growl while giving her undivided attention to each and
every candidate's surrogate campaigner, she loses time—and
traction—making her way throughout the house to reconnoiter
the roaming rascals from different windows. She is also leaving
nose prints in places where she doesn't commonly stare.

I digress.

I went and saw my postal worker, put on my best embarrassed face, and passed him the note from the principal. I told him my box number, and he came back with a bundle of garbage that would keep me warm for a week if I were to burn it all in the Vermont Castings ballot box.

I took my roll of ridiculousness and went to one of the lobby tables where I could adequately recycle everyone as I utilized the blue bin provided for my convenience. It has a slot specifically sized for cardboard campaign fliers.

I counted twenty-two of the pint-sized posters. Twenty-two! No party was unrepresented. All went into the hopper unread. I also received an L.L. Bean winter catalog and two or three *last* notices. Several were giving me my twenty-fifth final chance to get my car covered under an extended warranty, and one was an account statement from a local bank that's threatening to shut down one of my pitiful savings accounts.

Apparently, I *must* stop by and make a deposit or withdrawal within the next month. Seems the account has become inactive, and it must be costing time and money to keep my fifty-two dollars safe. They buy a stamp every single month to give me the warning. I opened the account to do some small-time investing in cryptocurrency. Don't ask me how that's going.

It was not lost on me that about half of the candidates represented by the overwhelming supply of paper-stock fliers would soon be demanding that I bring my own shopping bags to the grocery store. Soon, they will be asking me to leave the pickup truck home and take public transportation to my appointments. It won't be long before they are requesting money to fund more fliers for the campaign that will inevitably be the "most brutal" fight of their political career.

I pared my armload of mail down to three letters that had meaning. One was a Thanksgiving card from my camp neighbors thanking me for closing their cottage. That was nice. I received the title to an old motorcycle from the Maine Department of Motor Vehicles—I'd lost the other one.

I also received a bill for the copay for my recent medical examination. Now that I think of it, I should have asked the doctor to check for fliers while I was leaning over that table.

Ronnie on a Cliff

Of course, I know the ins-and-outs of my home, but this message from Ronnie the Roomba—while I was out for a black coffee and stale something-or-other—did concern me a bit.

"Ronnie is stuck on a cliff."

There are no cliffs in my home. This model of Roomba was programmed to back away from dangerous drop-offs. Up to this point, other than the Roomba completing a cleaning, or the battery dying when he got stuck behind a door, I had seen nothing dramatic in the messages I received. It's a robot, not a Kardashian.

Getting a Roomba for Christmas from my significant one was a strong message. She claimed that the house seemed dusty when she came by to visit. I agree; I typically blame the dog. I set up the notifications that allow the vacuuming robot to know when there was trouble.

Being named Timmy and watching many Lassie episodes in the '60s, you tend to try to interpret messages whenever you hear a dog barking with alarm. This text was much clearer, and I pictured a very dire situation.

I can't say as I ever thought I would be the guy getting messages from my vacuum cleaner, but I felt very connected as I careened toward Chez Timmay, wondering where my little cleaning buddy was stuck.

Come to find out, Ronnie had shut himself down as he had become stuck under the gas fireplace in the living room. I was a bit disappointed that the mishap was so minor. This is probably how June Lockhart felt when Lassie overstated how much danger Timmy was in. Let's be honest. The kid should have known better than to go near the well anyway.

My dog, Ellie, was unconcerned about the impending death of Ronnie as she has become quite adept at not giving a crap about the little round disc that sucks up—and subsequently collects—her ever-falling black hair.

She remained asleep with her stubby little boxer face hanging off the couch. The visible inner pinkness of her loose, whiskered cheeks rippled rhythmically as she took in just enough air to keep her alive until the next bowl of kibble was delivered.

Once I restarted Ronnie on his rounds, she opened one of her eyes and then moved ever so slightly to take advantage of the mobile rays of the warm sun as it wandered west across the sky and shined through her favorite bay window.

I just sat down and sipped the coffee slowly from the paper cup and watched Ellie sleep.

Some emergencies just aren't, are they?

SCAFFOLDING

NINETY-FIVE DEGREES WAS TWENTY-FIVE TOO MANY, BUT the previously borrowed construction scaffolding needed to be returned.

I know, many of you who lay your eyes on this little bit of scribbling are gifted the opportunity—each day—to see the magic of mercury manifesting itself as sweat upon your brow; ninety-five degrees is not welcome here.

I grabbed a trailer, a leaf-blower, and two bottles of cold water and headed east to dig it out from behind the shed at the camp. My buddy had been increasing the pressure on me, and he obviously needed it for a project at his house. Something about "Could I get my scaffolding back, maybe the next time you run to camp?"

I have to say, he had asked me to grab it about three, maybe four, times, and I kept forgetting to load it up on the way out of the woods. The past weekend I had intentions of bringing it home, but I realized the truck was full of other things. I determined that the next time I went to camp, I would get a trailer to make sure I could quickly load it up and return it promptly.

A few days ago, I called him to inquire if he was starting on the project this week or next. Not that it matters, but I wanted to make sure to be a responsible borrower and a responsible returner.

He told me that he could wait another week. Graduation festivities for his daughter were up in the queue, so he graced me with a little more time. I told him that if I could break free of the house for a few hours, I would make a special trip to camp, grab the staging, blow the leaves out of the neighbor's flower and fern beds, and then deliver it to him today.

He said, "No hurry. I think you've had at least four sections since 2007."

Do you know what? I think he was right. I surmised that I should have brought it back last year, maybe even in 2018.

I wasn't even mad at him for being a little pushy.

The stuff was in great shape; I hoped he wouldn't damage it. I would probably need to paint the trim boards and the eaves— again—next summer.

I'd drop it by his house today. I hoped he would be there to help me unload it.

If he could be as responsible a borrower as I had been, he would probably be able to deliver it to me the next time the scaffolding changed hands. I wouldn't even expect him to do it on a hot day. Sometime—in the early spring—would be fine.

September

I grabbed the two empty water jugs and trudged through the path lined by beech, hemlock, and pine. The grass between the tree roots and rocks swished against my boots and jeans, and I stopped whistling Earth, Wind & Fire's "September" for a few moments.

After being absent for most of the summer, the red squirrels had returned. This early absenteeism had been the topic of several conversations—most often, with my son. We discussed the uptick in hawk and owl sightings, and, during a couple of campfire colloquies, our theory was ready for publication. Standing there with empty plastic jugs, I realized that this needed more study. I should call him.

I chalked up the influx of fuzzy, red, tree devils in the upper branches of the beech trees to a banner year in crop production. Between the squirrels and the blue jays, the canopy of leaves had been abuzz with activity.

The jays scream and flap while squirrels chatter and scold. They all want the nuts, and they make it known.

I restarted my ruck toward the oasis where my water awaited. Due to the diligence of Canadian disc jockeys during my last listen to Sunday's playlist, I broke into a more vocal rendition of "September." *Ba de ya de ya de ya.* My faux falsetto was off by a mile, but my outside voice didn't bother a soul. I put up with the chattering and screaming of the wildlife, and they could deal with me.

I hit the gravel road and sauntered a few hundred yards to the empty clapboarded cottage. My summer neighbors had moved along as they abandoned Maine for far-western destinations. They left early this year; went to see family on the other coast for a time. I care for the place, opening and closing it so that they don't have to.

I repaired a few pipes, some lights, and a hand-carved wooden bird most recently. The wooden bird's perch is a pencil-thin wooden dowel, and it snapped after a four-foot drop. I suspected the cat, but he wasn't talking. My post-break proctology utilized a Milwaukee drill and a quarter-inch bit. Residue from the remainder of the rod was removed through rudimentary router-like action. A reglue made him good as new.

The water stays flowing through the camp until I judge those overnight temperatures demand a quick drain-down of the interior pipes. Last year I was a bit too late, and I had to put on my plumber's pants.

They let me fill my water jugs as partial payment for my mediocre service. I don't have a well at the lake. I use the vast cistern that sits in front of me for an endless supply of showers, but my drinking water comes from other sources. Viv's is a good one. Poland Spring should be so clear and tasteless. There is a cold-running spring at the front of my property, but hammer-driving a wellpoint has been put off for years. Someday, maybe.

I unlocked the place and entered the barren kitchen to find all the furniture covered in sheets. It's a far different piece of paradise at the height of summer. Nightly meals at the twelve-foot wooden slab of a table find me sitting in my regular spot enjoying Michelin three-star-level meals in the middle of the Maine woods at least a couple of times a week.

Being male—and alone much of the time—causes the mother/chef/friend in Viv to believe that I need feeding. My phone rings sometime around 3:00 o'clock on Friday afternoons.

"What time are you going to be here, because we can eat whenever you like."

"Viv, I'm gonna be a little late getting in, I had to pick up a (fill in the blank), and they didn't have any in stock. I must stop in Ellsworth. Sammy is with me, too."

"You bring him, of course. I made more than enough. Just come when you boys get to the camp. We have three different desserts, and Bob made pork roast."

"We will be there around 5:30."

We stay until it's well after dark, and we feel our way back to camp, counting our steps in and on the gravel road until we guess where to turn onto the path back to my place. An occasional branch whacks me in the face. The inadvertent minor ankle sprain in a newly created chipmunk hovel creates word strings not fit for dear mother's ears.

Once through the trees, after scuffing your feet along the route to avoid tripping over the same old roots, we finally see the glow of the lamp that I left on for Ellie.

Viv's place was cold and empty. But the view from the kitchen— where Bob washes the endless dirty dinner dishes—is the same. I filled my jugs, locked up, and wandered slowly back to my place. I stopped to speak directly to the chipmunk, who was still cleaning the last of the summer's Virginia peanuts off the red-painted porch.

"You're lucky, little fella. Viv is still feeding you!"

I trudged back with the two jugs filled to maximum capacity. Up the gravel road, a quick left down the path by Everett's place—he was back in Rhode Island—and then over the roots and rocks that cause me trouble on all the walks back in the dark. I broke into my outside voice again, and none of the wildlife ceased their work; it was September after all.

> *There was a ba de ya, say do you remember,*
> *ba de ya, dancing in September*
> *ba de ya. Never was a cloudy day.*

Shades of February Darkness

The shades of February darkness were yanked down quickly as I attempted to reread *Moby Dick* under the illumination of a yellowing map light in the Green Glider.

The Green Glider is the name of the 1999 CRV that I use for winter travel. It's not pretty, but it runs like new. Only rust will be its Grim Reaper as time progresses and body panels become mere suggestions.

Potholes and asphalt, as broken as the dreams of the men who also sit nearby, are sure to compress the original struts into giving up one day. But not yet; not today.

I'll run GG until it no longer takes an inspection sticker, then I will bring in professionals to patch it up one more time.

Old eyes were no help in slowly deciphering and savoring Melville's magnificent missive. I put the book down on the salt-stained carpet to begin to gaze upon the chaotic stage that is a poorly lit parking lot on a Saturday evening in Maine.

The parking jobs were delicious to watch, as lounge-pant-clad ladies and gents pulled in diagonally more than perpendicular in order to grab one last thing before settling onto couches, chairs, and carpet-covered hardwood floors of their respective homes and apartments.

A man with a limp, a young girl running with a box of Orville Redenbacher popcorn, and a woman grunting to heave two cases of spring water into the bed of a Ford pickup truck while her husband played on his phone were the first act. I applauded their commitment.

I was not a critic, but merely an audience member with comped tickets given to me by my visitor, who, for some reason, believes that milk should not be kept past the expiration date. She also pointed out that the Chips Ahoy Reese's Cup-filled cookies are not appropriate snack foods for the soon-to-arrive blonde bombshell who goes by the name of "G-daughter."

I know what she likes, and the cookies were not discarded, only counted to ensure that my story was not fabricated to allow me to ingest more than one—or two—of the new wave of Nabisco staple food.

As a kid, I could only dream of such confectionery delights. Chocolate chips were enough for me because I knew of nothing else. This genetically modified delivery system for all that is good and holy in the candy world is just unbelievable. Dreams do come true.

Soon, the out-of-town lady known for travel was ejected from the store with a buggy full of healthy choices and a quart of soymilk. I had to leave my theater seating to load the bags that felt far too heavy to be carbohydrates. There was roughage and whole grains afoot, and I was taken hostage in my own car for the ride home with the playwright of "You Can't Take It with You." Moss Hart would be disappointed in what we have done to the audience.

SINGLE SHELF STORAGE SOLUTIONS AND SUSHI

MY SIGNIFICANT OTHER—CURRENTLY LIVING A SEMI-charmed kind of nomadic professional life—settled in for some "Hey, TC, I'm in-between places" time at Casa de Timmaay.

This is not difficult unless you, the full-time dweller of the 1966 vintage stick-built emporium of the unopen concept, have placed all your things on the shelves in a bathroom built for one. I don't do hair and makeup, but she does. I must say that she pulls it off nicely, but she needs a steamer trunk for storage of the supplies; I just don't have room for it all.

I have a comb, a brush, a couple of partially filled plastic floss boxes, one-eighth of one ounce of aftershave, two pairs of fingernail clippers (one of them is industrial grade for toenails that argue at times), two sticks of Old Spice deodorant, tooth-paste, a couple of pairs of tweezers for controlling the eyebrows that were originally designed for winter-dwelling sasquatches, and, of course, an electric toothbrush—Oh, and a razor; manual shift, no clutch. I can fit all of it on one shelf, but I had spread it around, partially covering each of the same three surfaces. It seemed like a good idea. It looked very sparse, and I felt good about my storage solutions.

With her move from the south to a more northern city (it would still be considered south to anyone from Maine) came some transition time. I have just determined why my back hurts when I shuttle her and the bags back and forth to Bangor's International Airport. The potions and lady-like named prod-ucts that litter my sparse man domain have me so confused. I have more ladies' names in front of me than could ever have been one-handedly scratched upon the walls of the men's locker room at the Brewer bowling lanes back in the early '70s.

Who are these women, and why are their bottles of product so large? We have argued about it for a couple of weeks. She won, of course. We have had fun with it. She claims she will take most of the scientifically developed containers (of lady-in-a-bottle) with her when her new place opens up.

I am praying—daily—that her new bathroom is large and designed well after Mike Brady retired from his firm in southern California.

This is nothing new, but I had forgotten what it was like living with a lady. It's been almost three years to the day from when I assisted in her move to regions on the southern coast of these here United States. In that time, she has learned to enjoy semispicy foods and southern barbeque. She took me to a few spots during my limited visits to her bachelorette pad. I enjoyed it very much.

Her bathroom was much more spacious than ours, so my shaving kit could sit right on the counter and never be bumped and subsequently dumped.

Before she heads back out the door via air, I promised to introduce her to good sushi. Yes, we have that in Maine.

She wasn't up for a meal of compressed rice, raw fish, and delicious seaweed before her last jaunt, but now she wants me to give her some simple lessons in the art of mixing wasabi with soy sauce for the perfect bit of zing on raw tuna.

I'll do that, of course. I am pretty handy with chopsticks; believe it or not. Something about eating with shards of wood (and not spilling much) makes me feel like I could go to the big city and be less wide-eyed when entering citified sushi joints. I might whittle a couple of my own sticks from white birch.

Sleeping on the Swinging Bed

I don't typically sleep on the rope-slung bed. It's reserved for the Significant One. While the little lady had slipped into Maine at a reasonable hour, her bags had spent the evening at JFK. She made a call to the woods to inform me that she would not be making the trek to camp as she was low on raiment and other things.

While it was a hot day, the north wind had other plans for the evening feature presentation. I opened the windows after dark and let the sounds of the rolling water and whistling wind fill up the porch. I took advantage of the free chill and dragged my dunnage to the porch, made up the bed with a sleeping bag, and enough pillows to decorate the davenports of three grannies.

Slumped and swinging, I slept like a sloth who'd broken into a barrel of bourbon.

I picked up a passenger for my ride through slumberland at around 2:00. She did well. contorting around most of my frame. That changed at first light. The furry one determined that sitting up and watching for interlopers was the reason for her adoption.

She pivots—frequently—for a better view of the moat and surrounding forest. This moves the bed a bit too much for comfortable slugging around. The bird strike on the north-facing windows created a crescendo of claws on the dusty pine board floor as she investigated and barked an official report.

I rose, with much scratching and displeasure, to find that the bird had flown away—unaffected—from the numbing blow to its noggin. Birds are tough, FYI.

I gave up, made coffee, walked out to my septic tank project to make mental calculations about the necessities that would be needed to finish up. I wanted to make only one trip to the supply depot, but that was probably not a realistic expectation.

So goes a late summer slumber on the jagged edge of America.

SUMMER DREAMS

SUMMER DREAMS OF SIMPLE FIXES ON OLD OUTBOARD MO-tors and bug-free relaxification—while slumped in cedar-slat chairs—had taken a turn for the worse. Instead, I'd been forced to seek help from boat-motor professionals, and I was stung by more than one wasp while shooing squirrels from the shed.

Expectations can turn to disappointment the minute that you feel your dreams will be overpowered by life's realities.

Nope, I'm not broken, busted, crushed, or in any way depressed. Fifty-seven years of well-delivered lessons have kept me grounded. That causes me to loosely stuff life's dunnage in my backpack of expectations. Always pack dreams with a bit of extra room for bigger plans. It also allows for the addition of unexpected and last-minute problems and barriers.

Karma waits until you are busy looking for your keys before stuffing the side pockets of your pack.

Keep your pack close—possibly closed. Tell the leading players in your life that your backpack is full, and you'll help them carry some stuff, but you've already got plenty of your own.

Sometimes, you need a little break. Don't be afraid to let people know.

The Extra Step

It's not a big deal, but I appreciate her.

Over the last month and a half, I have found myself rooting around the city for a quick lunch on most days. I am usually in the company of one or two people when we determine that it's time to go out to grab a bite.

There are a bunch of great sandwich shops in Bangor. There are plenty of choices for burgers, pizza, Italian food, Mexican fare, Chinese cuisine, and—when I want a cup of chili—we usually go to Wendy's.

You see, one of the locations where I learned to punch a clock was at Wendy's on Hogan Road in Bangor. It's a story not unlike every other American kid who needed money for gas, school clothes, date-night money, and the occasional cassette tape of my favorite album. I worked at several fast-food restaurants.

While it is frowned upon by everyone who says they love me, I am a lover of Coca-Cola. I don't keep it at home much, as water has taken over the soft-drink shelf in my fridge. It was not my decision, so there is no need to praise my healthy choices; it was forced upon me. I try to comply.

However, when I have a burger or chili, I like Coca-Cola.

Please don't send me notes to berate me for my love of Coca-Cola. I understand it's not in one of the food groups, but I am not taking applications for a personal dietician.

I digress.

This is not about Coke; it's about the lady at the window.

Most commonly, I am the driver of the plain black SUV with the hidden blue lights, so I am the person who interacts with the folks at the drive-up window. On multiple occasions, the lady at the Union Street Wendy's location passes our bags of food out to the hungry crew, but not before she passes me my Coke.

I noted that she always inspects the cup, and inevitably she locates a drop or two of Coca-Cola that is dripping down the side of the cup. It is fast food, and they have a pretty good cadence going as they move the food from grill to shelf, from shelf to bag, and from window to hungry customers.

I've pulled up to my fair share of drive-up windows in my time, and it seems that I usually get handed a wet cup. It's not a big deal, but I typically ask for an extra napkin to avoid sticking to the next thing I need to touch or grab.

She is not a young woman. She is probably very close to my age. She inspects each cup, and before it meets her passing standard, she uses a clean damp cloth to wipe down the sides. She then passes me the drink, and I can tell by her eyes that she is smiling. Masks put a curse on the easiest way to spot a friendly face, but her eyes are clear and bright. Trust me. She's smiling.

For the course of the summer, I noticed her care for my cups. I mentioned to the deputy chief that I appreciated the fact that she cared enough to wipe down the cups. I might have said that I was a pretty good drive-thru worker in my day, but I never even thought to wipe down the cups.

The conversation turned to work ethic, concern for others, and doing the best job that you can do even when no one is watching.

Last week, I did what I have wanted to do many times. I took the cup, and I told her how much I appreciated her time and effort in wiping down my soft drink cups throughout the summer. I just said, "I've noticed you always do that, and I appreciate it. I just wanted you to know that not many people would take the time to do that."

She just smiled and nodded. I felt like a heavy weight had been lifted off my shoulders. I just needed to say it. I am sure she wipes off everyone's cup. She's that kind of person.

Many people around us take extra steps, but we are all moving so fast that sometimes we don't notice them.

It makes me want to try harder to be the type of person who wipes the cup. I probably won't succeed every time, but I should try harder.

We can all do better. It's not a big deal, but I appreciate her efforts; at least now she knows.

The Fall Collection

Being limited in my summer wardrobe choices, the continued downward trend in morning wake-up temperatures had reopened a whole new world of options for me.

When I say new, I really mean old but more plentiful.

You see, a mope from Maine doesn't get carried away grabbing excessive stacks of fashionable summer wear. You have a stash, but keeping too much stock of lightweight, wispy shirts is unnecessary. You are never more than four months away from putting them into the back of the closet.

If you live north of Augusta (that's in the center of the state), summer is short and so is your supply of shirts with sleeves that identify as less than long.

Oh, but the heavyweight chambray, mid-weight flannel, and the subsequent heavier flannel and chamois shirt collections are plentiful and ready to come out of mothballs by mid- to late September. They won't need to be stuffed into storage until the end of April.

My commute to work is only about three to four good songs, so the shirts surely don't get worn out. The second change of the day is into a uniform, so there is no worry of putting too many miles on the long-sleeved fall selections. It's a collection that looks much the same as last year's fall collection and is remarkably like the offerings from the year before. I daresay there will be few drastic changes for autumn of next year, but what do I know? There might be a sale.

Someone is sure to ask, "TC, why don't you just wear a uniform to work and skip the changing the second time?" Good question, but for many reasons wearing a uniform to and from work is frowned upon, and it should be. There is a myriad of reasons why it's not a good idea, so I'll just say that flannel is fine for the journey to and from, and I have plenty. It's nice to blend in wearing a cotton blend.

On lazy days, once it becomes cold enough, a hoodie will suffice. No one is judging me on the runway. I'd lose miserably if they were.

I rediscovered a pack of gum left over from April in the front pocket of my ratty Carhartt sweatshirt. I had to throw it on when I wandered to the shed to look for a bottle of lower unit gear oil for servicing the outboard motors. I found the oil, and my breath was minty fresh during the search.

It was time to winterize the boats that allowed us to let our summer sleeves flap in the warm winds of what seems like the shortest season of the year. I'm good with it. Mornings are more pleasant with a shiver. I think I have just the shirt for that.

THE HIERARCHY OF RIDING SHOTGUN

DECISIONS ABOUT WHO GETS TO RIDE "SHOTGUN" ON A CAR trip are not as straightforward as one might think. Anyone with a few miles under their seat belt should understand that a myriad of factors determines who gets to ride in the front passenger seat. Everyone comes from a different place and a different set of standards in selecting the seat.

In the early years, calling out "shotgun" to ride in the front passenger seat was completely acceptable. It was a point rarely argued among close friends, and if you were not a close friend, you already knew better than calling out the word "shotgun." In reality, it is in no way as simple as calling out "shotgun"—and it shouldn't be.

For most of my life, at least since my teen years, it was pretty clear how the position is determined. Factors include physical condition, physical build, age, relationship with the driver, number of people traveling, number of seats available, marital status with the operator, and the list goes on and on. The onset of motion sickness for a person who rides in the back can override many other factors. Most of us do not carry barf bags. We really should.

The rules of engagement were learned through watching older siblings taking control during the sprints to the front seat. Their calls of "front seat" meant the same thing.

As the lone male in my cast of siblings, I had to contend with two older sisters—one to block and one to lay down some smack. The older sister would give verbal clues about how it was going to work. These less-than-subtle hints would be backed up with low levels of violence if, perchance, I was to make it to the front seat before she did.

She had ulterior motives in her quest for the front seat of the 1965 Biscayne. What she wanted was absolute control of both the front seat and the radio knobs. She was a totalitarian Dick Clark.

The czar of the shotgun seat would use my other sister as the strong arm. If the elder was not available to travel, who would be in front was obvious. At that time of my life, I had no desire to control the radio.

While growing up, both parents usually accompanied us in the car. In that case, the war cry in the Cotton driveway was, "I got a window." Yes, we used that terminology, and while the statement is grammatically incorrect, it did not matter. The message was clear; I would be stuck in the middle of the back-seat. Even if I called out the words, I still had to contend with the stratum of my position in the household.

I might try to open the door in a chivalrous move to indicate that one of the sisters should get in first. Violence would ensue, and I would be manhandled or, in this case, woman-handled and forced into the car like the secret service when they are attempting to protect a candidate or dignitary. It happened fast, and, before you knew it, I no longer had a window. I stopped calling out the phrase after a time. Why waste the energy?

In the end, the hierarchy of calling shotgun is learned through a series of lessons. You might gain control of the shotgun seat by birthright, force, or manipulation. Calling shotgun is not always the deciding factor on where you end up riding in a vehicle.

As you can imagine, yelling the word "shotgun" when on duty can cause some concern among the officers in the immediate vicinity. We don't do that. And since we don't ride three or four to a car, we always have a window. At this point in my life, I am pretty happy with that.

The Old Apple Tree

The landscape of beautiful, wet, white, and windblown snow belied the damage done to the formerly upright citizens in our more forested areas.

A late-afternoon drive after the violent storm revealed mauled maples, bashed beech, toppled poplars, and stately spruces now sporting an unexpected trim.

Birches bowed down as if to welcome an unexpected and overweight guest who'd perched on their leafless branches with demands that only a late-afternoon sunbeam could force their eviction.

Trees who had hidden internal decay with a cheap suit of bark were soon determined to be down and out. It pays to have a good tailor, but a cheap suit can't hide the truth from a relentless and robust wind.

If you asked me which fallen tree branches make me feel the most sorrowful, I would have to say it is the gnarled limbs of the centuries-old apple tree.

Disheveled rock walls that run like hard, gray rivers throughout forgotten New England boundary lines are at their best when they are guarded by old apple trees.

While following the remnants of an ancient rock wall, who hasn't found all forward motion stopped by the dark tentacles of a lonely apple tree?

He stands like a wrinkled and stubborn old man who refuses to leave his neighborhood despite the incoming yuppies represented by the fir and hardwood families.

If the lifecycle is right, he still provides small red or green apples for the four-legged neighborhood kids who frolic on and in the stone fortress he guards. Standing still and watching him for a time allows you to see twinkling eyes that hide a story or two for those willing to stop and listen.

The fallen branches will find a way to warm us again. Chopped and split, they will be stacked by sturdy Mainers who will honor them by returning them to ashes next winter.

Summer travelers will be able to buy bundles of the fallen from the roadside firewood stands so that they can warm their hands from the 2.2-mile hike while enjoying marshmallows toasted from the heat of a one-hundred-year-old apple tree. They will never appreciate the stubborn way he went down or hear the stories he could tell when forced to defend himself from a forceful north wind.

The birches? Some will straighten, and some will snap. It is a cycle that cannot be stopped.

We hope that we can remain, at least as long as the old apple tree. We want to share our stories and be hopeful that our eyes twinkle when we tell tales to the neighborhood kids. But even the sturdy apple tree doesn't last forever.

The Rain

The canopy of leaves slowed the descent of the rain-drops to the point that they merely tapped—ever so lightly—on the shingles.

If you were inclined to make a comparison—and I am—you might liken it to the manner that a neighbor knocks when they really don't want you to come to the cookout later that afternoon; they only tap to say that they tried.

What the neighbor didn't know is that you pulled the covers over your head so that you could relay to them, later, that you were there, but you didn't hear them. Passive aggressiveness is a great equalizer, and the raindrops were just like that.

In any event, the rain softens the prospect for the day ahead. The things that need to be done can be put off without any measurable guilt.

Rain is a reason not to mow the lawn because it really needs a day to dry out.

Rain is a willing dance partner to a book that needs to be finished. If the rain is relentless, she may allow you to start another.

Rain is a liquid excuse that doesn't require you to explain your failure to those who expected more from you.

I like the rain.

The Scent of a Woman (Not the Movie)

The odor is strong. It is a cross between New York extrasharp cheddar, Garnier Fructis Color Shield shampoo (it's paraben-free), and a bucket of white perch left behind under an aluminum boat seat in mid-July.

While the added detail of the material used to construct the boat might not be necessary for you to know, the reflective qualities of unpainted aluminum do magnify the sun's rays to a level that could quickly bake a tray of buttermilk biscuits to a golden-brown hue. You should smell what it can do to a bucket of perch.

Initially, when she returned from her walk, she rushed by, heading toward her water dish. I suppose that mouthwash wasn't on her mind, but it should have been. I was standing on a stepladder, well above the fray, and the odiferous invisible wall of stink wafted up to my nasal passages from at least four feet below.

Sammy had taken her for a walk. She had been cooped up in the camp while I slowly installed a series of electrical outlets to the screened-in porch. She sat at the door and whined while I drilled oblong holes through the wall studs to run the 12/2 wire. It makes you sad to hear a dog longing to be outside, but I didn't want her to get into something if she wandered off, unsupervised.

I'd seen a couple of porcupines in the vicinity, and I know she has the heart of an investigator. I didn't have any desire to pull out quills while trying to keep her under control. She is a strong dog.

Ellie tends to stay within the line of sight, but she also knows when it is time to—subtly—fade out of view. At that point, her hearing becomes very spotty. It must be the thick forestation that blocks the friendly "come-hithers."

I sometimes resort to a bit of yelling. Often, I do some searching and hiking, but there are moments when I just slam the truck door a couple of times. The sound of someone leaving without her company has a healing effect on her eardrums. So far, we have avoided a trip to the audiologist. Dog audiologists are expensive; at least, that's what I have heard.

Sammy—Ellie's bestest friend—took her out for a saunter and swim. He said that he spotted the not-so-fresh pile of something dead upon the rocks by the water. He surmised that a member of the weasel family had shredded some formerly swimming soul into a pile of postmortem perfume. The sun-baked rock turned the pile o' leavings into Ellie's latest eau de toilette water with a strong emphasis on toilette.

His story—and I believe him—was that Ellie first moistened her black hide with a frigid dip. Once she reached the perfect level of fur hydration, she exited the water and quickly made her way to roll in the pile of whatever she smells like now. She favors using her face as a probe when she is rolling around in dead things. Understandably, the face is located on the end of the dog where I spend most of my time. It made sense, however, that the opposite end of this dog currently smelled much better. No, I did not double-check.

Sammy tried some Dawn dish detergent on her muzzle and melon, but it merely caused us to sense a stronger level of stink. We put her out on the porch to dry, but that's where I was. It seems that heat—and stink—rises, and I was on the ladder.

Once I completed the electrical endeavor, I went to the shower room and selected the only shampoo currently available on this jagged edge of America—unless I decided to drive into town for something more powerful. Yes, I used the Fructis, but I would have used any shampoo left behind in the shower by the official owner.

Ellie and I wandered to the shore and waded in. Spring-fed lakes tend to warm slowly. Certainly, we did not expect it to be warm in May. Still, it's shocking to a man—and maybe a woman—but Ellie seemed to take the temperature in stride. I began to scrub her as well as I could with no collar present to grasp. She is a pretty obedient dog, but she did not want to stick around for the full-Fructis-and-cold-water soaking treatment.

The scrubbing was a sideshow. Sammy watched from the porch. I did my best while managing to keep my nether regions from dipping too deeply into the clear and cold cleanser of weasel—or otter—condiments.

I'd make a joke of singing soprano, but it's overused in similar situations. Suffice it to say that I felt a slight tingle. I sensed a smile on Ellie's fully Fructis-foamed face as she pulled toward deeper water so that she could rinse thoroughly.

Drying off was typical mayhem, like that which occurs when drying off any noncompliant four-legged beast. You have lived it. I don't need to explain.

The trip home was pleasant enough with the windows rolled down. By the judicious opening of the driver's side window, one can create a crossflow of scent if you open the passenger's side rear window a bit more. It's science.

Ellie didn't seem to be bothered by the faces I made in the rearview mirror. Most involved the scrunching of my abnormally large nose along with guttural sounds that indicated that I was about to pull over to wretch on the roadside.

The following day, as Ellie soaked up the sun in her bay window of choice, I noted that the ceiling fan was moving the air around as expected. Once her black fur came up to temperature, there was a strong and fruity rotten-fish odor that lingered nicely. I pulled the curtains to keep the sun from baking her fur any further.

I had placed her long-loved fluorescent orange collar in a plastic bag. Once I opened the bag, it allowed a bit more of the sour smell of death to drift through the house. I removed her nametag, and I tossed the old collar deep into the garbage.

I drove into town for a new collar. Fully believing that I had some powerful scent-removing shampoo under the kitchen sink, I skipped buying from the display of miraculous elixirs that guarantee a scent-free dog. That was an oversight.

When I returned home from work on Monday night, I found that the house had been ravaged further by the stink of the beast. More scrubbing was necessary, and we managed to knock the stench back a bit more. I did not have a pleasant dog-centric odor-enhancing shampoo on hand, so I kicked it old-school.

Ellie was later spritzed with a bit of water-diluted Dolce & Gabbana "The One." I rarely spritz myself with store-bought attractants, but it's good to have a bottle of it around in case your dog takes on the odor of fish—in this case, dead fish.

Now the house smelled like the foyer of a Caribbean Island casino on "All You Can Eat Fried Grouper Night," right after the recently docked cruise-ship customers spent ninety bucks on duty-free cologne.

Man! I was feeling lucky.

THE TOUCH

HE WALKED INTO THE HOUSE AND WAS IMMEDIATELY OVER-
whelmed by the smell of stale cigarettes. No one smoked in
this house; the odor was stowed away—invisibly—in the fi-
bers of the dark blue uniform. He went directly to the basement, scuffed across the cold floor, and then pulled the chrome
beaded chain to turn on the incandescent lightbulb dangling
over the Kenmore.

He could always catch the chain on the first grab in the
darkness. It had become a mental challenge, but he kept it to
himself. No one would understand, so why inform anyone that
he made small wagers with himself before he reached for it.

"If I catch it on the first grab, I will treat myself to a large
coffee tomorrow morning, right after I pick up the mail."

Reaching for a thin chain in the pitch black of a window-
less cellar had become his way of determining that his hand
was still steady. It was a gauge to find if his coordination and
ability to make accurate mental estimates were still up to par.
He caught it perfectly.

He missed the chain on the first grab two years and
three months ago. He later learned that she had pulled it too
quickly—or too hard—before leaving the dank laundry room
with a basket filled with clean sheets. The recoil of that snap
had launched the small glass crystal at the end of the chain over
the protruding brass pull on the cupboard door where the Tide
and dryer sheets were stored.

That night, he felt panic when he missed. Had he finally
lost it? He flailed around repeatedly, swiping his hand through

the black humid air—no chain! Was it broken? Had he miscounted the seventeen evenly spaced steps across the uneven basement floor? He grabbed repeatedly and comically. When his hand found the drooping loop, he pulled it so hard that the ornamental glass knob struck him square in the eye. The light came on.

He skipped the coffee the next day. A bet is a bet, and he'd lost.

It had been a long shift—fourteen hours. The cop knew that the uniform had to be thrown into the washing machine immediately. This would minimize the odors carried into his safe space. His house was a refuge from the stinky—smokey—places that he had recently visited, sometimes uninvited, on his patrol shift.

He threw the indigo uniform—filled with the odors of bad habits and poor decisions—into the thirty-six-year-old washer. It made noises that would not be considered normal, but it worked just fine.

She would ask him for a new washing machine again, soon. The ancient machine was dented and scratched. It was his first. It had become a challenge to keep it running. When she came along, she had changed all the furniture, the curtains, and the flooring, even the menu; he'd kept his washer.

He kicked a wedge of an old cedar shingle deeper under the front right corner. He muttered, "That'll steady you. You won't be keeping me awake." The Kenmore fought back but complied with his wishes. This could change without warning.

A quick shower and a cursory search of the fridge contents revealed nothing unusual or suspicious. He looked at the clock while he cleaned up the leftover guacamole with a couple of stale saltines.

"0327 hours." He could sleep for four hours if he went to bed right now. He brushed his teeth again. There was no reason to breathe fire into her face when he climbed into bed. He was sure that the garlic was better than the old cigarette smoke that was now being mechanically and chemically scrubbed out of his uniform. He heard the old machine knocking like an angry upstairs neighbor. The wedge must have moved again.

He slipped into the bed like a well-starched—stumbling—apparition. He groped for the remote and recovered it near the middle of the bed. He held it with the full intention of finding an infomercial about coated baking pans that were easy to clean no matter how long you left burned cheese in the bottom.

He thought about cheese for a few minutes. He had no control over the pre-dream thought process. He knew it made no sense, but it felt like the right thing to ponder. He could hear Dobie Gray's smooth tones as "Drift Away" eclipsed the thoughts of crispy cheese on the bottom of a copper pan. Sleep would be coming soon.

He took a deep breath, and then he felt it. It happened every time, usually within three to five minutes of entering the well-broken-in Western king. There was the touch. It is not spoken about—often—within police circles, but he knew it was not uncommon. It was one of the most basic reassurances displayed between the members of a family unit.

The touch most often comes when a formerly sleeping spouse reaches delicately across to make sure that their slumber has been disturbed because their partner has made it home. The touch has never been taught, nor was it ever talked about. It needs no instruction, no written directions. The touch just happens, and it happens for good reasons.

Dark days followed by short nights have made the touch symbolic yet gratifying. It is different for each one of us, yet it is done for the same reasons no matter where you are in the world.

Her voice broke the silence of the dark room, "Did you eat the guacamole?"

He stroked her hand and turned his head toward the wall. He knew he had consumed too much garlic.

He closed his eyes and focused more on Dobie Gray and less on the burned cheese. The song always started on the second verse when he was worn out. He felt like he was humming the melody, but it was probably just part of the dream.

"Beginning to think that I'm wastin' time
I don't understand the things I do.
The world outside looks so unkind,
So I'm countin' on you to carry me through."

Another day, another bet, another successful grab at the beaded chrome chain. He would have his coffee. First, he would sleep.

Postscript

"The Touch" is introspective, and only partially autobiographical. Many of the thoughts and actions are taken from my own life, but some are borrowed from the lives of others. It's part of a series of essays that encompass a tapestry of police officers that I have known through the thirty-four years on the job. It's still one of my favorites, and it evokes strong emotions when I read it. It's probably because I have lived much of it, but also because some of the thoughts and points were gleaned from officers who are no longer with us. I don't dwell on loss, but loss sometimes visits you late at night, usually uninvited.

THREE O'CLOCK EPIPHANY

MY THREE O'CLOCK EPIPHANY IS BROUGHT TO YOU BY THE shadowy outline of a black dog with ears perked in a manner that makes you believe she is about to ask a question. She doesn't; she just continues to stare until you begin to question all your own life choices.

While you know she is a kind animal, you wonder if she is contemplating a turn to violence to wake you from your slumber. She remains silent.

She may have listened to the multitude of Miranda warnings broadcast daily from the flat screen in the living room; I leave it on for her. Maybe the endless viewing of *Criminal Minds*—while you are away—has allowed this seventy-three-pound dog to collect hundreds of examples of deviant behavior, poisonings, shootings, stabbings, and, of course, stalking one's prey.

For some reason, I believe the solace of the human voices that come out of the electronic window might be comforting to her. But—instead—she might be learning the ways of man.

This dog's refusal to answer questions gives off the vibe that she has an attorney on retainer. She keeps secrets and has learned too much. She believes your investigatory skills don't hold a candle to those of Joe Mantegna.

Still, she stares. She controls her breathing; she keeps in mind that the spring shedding of her winter coat leaves physical evidence all over the house. She recalls that no one—not one person—on that show has ever questioned the dog.

I am sure that she wonders why no one has ever asked where the dog was on the night of the crime.

I make the mistake of moving. Sure, it was only a slight change of position that a mere mortal would never notice, but she does. Ears perk higher, her front feet begin to lift and drop as if she is about to break into a delightful dance.

I silently pray for dawn, but it might be too late by morning's light. I reach out from under the warm comforter to touch and test the dark void between her muzzle and mine. I recoil when I feel the cool, moist nose of a creature who is driving me to madness with her patience. My eyes strain through the fog of inky darkness to make sure she has no weapons.

She must have come in peace, this time. I rise to fumble and tumble into something appropriate for post-evening wear. I find that a sweatshirt—still inside-out when I see myself in the bathroom mirror—is the only available option.

It seems she only wants to go outside—this time—but what about next time? Her patience is maddening. Upon returning to the house, I unscrew the top of the Milk-Bone jar. It's something she has not mastered, and she has no thumbs.

I crawl back into bed and pull the covers up to my neck a little tighter. Ellie settles nearby, in a place where I cannot see her eyes. She finally begins to snore, and I feel comfortable enough to fall back asleep, but only for now. I know this will happen again. I am hopeful she appreciated the biscuit.

I'll leave the television tuned to one of the shopping networks from now on. I will secure my credit card in the safe. I don't believe that she knows the combination.

Throwing Snow for the Dog

It was a lovely morning on the jagged edge of the continent. I'd be inclined to call the overnight snow totals just a minor annoyance. I surmised through standard investigatory methods that we had received about five inches.

The problem is the snow was saturated. It was similar to the soggy newspaper delivered by an unscrupulous and uncaring paperboy who delivers in a monsoon without an umbrella.

As I shoveled a path to the dooryard, Ellie staged herself perfectly to practice her acting skills. She pretended to fall victim to the perfectly projected precipitation.

Standing on her hind legs and flailing her front paws in the air to pretend that she was being tormented by low-flying lumps of snow made her feel that she was part of the process. She was fun to watch, but she barked loud enough to wake a distant neighbor.

Still, her vocalization was slightly muffled when she got a dense dose directly in the mouth. She sneezed it away and came back for more. It almost looked like she was smiling, and that, in turn, made me smile.

Smiling makes the twinges of pain in the lumbar region far more acceptable; nine out of ten doctors agree. The lone standout is a chiropractor who has you on a weekly adjustment schedule.

Even in the pitch black of a 3:35 morning wake-up, her dark body running across a background of ivory white snow created the illusion that I was watching a monochromatic masterpiece of filmmaking. It appeared to have been created by a second-year film student who discovered that shooting a movie in black and white could earn them a pat on the back from third-year film students who already passed that stage on their way to becoming the next Quentin Tarantino.

TOMATOES

I HAD BEEN PLUCKING TOMATOES. THE RED RASCALS APPEARED to be multiplying overnight on my mother's plants.

We could take a lesson from how tomatoes quietly decide to ripen at their own pace. You never hear them argue about it, and it doesn't appear that they are upset with each other when one of them makes it to the optimum size and color before the rest of the group.

It seems that some of them transition directly from green to red in unison. Many of them don't.

It's almost like they discuss it after dark. Maybe there's a vote?

Sunny kitchen windowsills are a fine finishing school reserved for those from the plant who are slow to mature. It might be one of the last bastions of true acceptance.

"Oh, you might be green now, but spend a little time with this little group of slower learners, and you'll be in the big dinner salad in no time. You can do it!"

Everyone figures it out at a different pace.

It's probably good that tomatoes avoid most social media channels. We don't need online arguments to ruin peaceful and productive vegetable gardens.

Sometimes the tomatoes appear to be better citizens than the rest of us. If you stand way back, remain silent, and leave them alone, you could learn a lot from a tomato.

Turning Back Time

CONTRARY TO POPULAR OPINION—AND THE WELL-PRACTICED words from semiattractive humans on the television who inform us about all the big stories in our news cycle—you do not gain time by setting your clocks back in the fall.

The amount of daylight you will receive has much more to do with what time you choose to get out of bed. If you think darkness causes humankind to become dormant, you should come ride with us.

Let's face it, you probably won't be able to sleep in. Your kids will still want a bowl of Froot Loops, and the dog is going to sniff your face until you let her out.

Sleeping-in ended when you were seventeen. Incidentally, that was the same period that your birthday no longer mattered to anyone but your mother. You know your dad sure isn't sending you a card.

Sure, Facebook has made birthdays "a thing," but it merely forces the polite among us to click on the button that sends a Happy Birthday message; it's not heartfelt. If it was, we'd send a gift.

This, in turn, forces you to write, "Thank you, so much, for all the birthday wishes yesterday. It means so much to have a group of friends who remember my birthday."

Let's face it, if you hadn't given Zuckerberg your date of birth in your Facebook profile only one person would remember your birthday. Maybe two if you count your significant other. Chances are, if that's a man, we are back to one; that's your mother.

For those of you working nightshifts all over the planet—nurses, docs, cops, factory workers, doughnut makers, and criminals—no one in payroll really knows whether or not you get paid for the extra hour when we set the clocks back, so don't ask. It'll all work out.

No, I did not mention firefighters in my list of night workers. I'm still angry that I didn't follow in my grandfather's footsteps and pick a job that supplies a bed at work.

And, for you firefighters, I've already heard the jokes about cops only becoming cops because they scored too low on the civil service exam. This is a valid point, and well taken. I cannot argue with you. You won; you're right.

So, set your clocks back one hour. Hug a firefighter. Wish someone a happy birthday before Zuck mentions it.

VALENTINE

VALENTINE'S DAY WAS A BIZARRE CELEBRATION IF YOU WERE in elementary or grammar school in the '60s and '70s.

I only remembered—this morning—about the decorated paper bag "mailboxes" we hung up in our classrooms to become the recipients of mandatory notes of adoration.

Along with the memory came the recollection that I always hated doing that.

This event had to have been contrived by someone who sold greeting cards. It was like being stuck in a Hallmark reeducation camp run by Mrs. Hutchinson, who probably deserved at least one Valentine's card.

Oh, and she could have used some breath mints.

Still, we forget. Not our love for that significant special person, but to buy the card, send the flowers, and say the sweet nothings.

If there was a life lesson in all that late-night card signing before the big day in fourth grade, it indeed slipped the mind of every man that I stand shoulder-to-shoulder with in the CAOR (Crowded Aisle of Ruins) that *is* the Valentine's Day card section at every big-box pharmacy across this great nation.

We join the mass male exodus from office and garage bay; usually, it's late in the day on the 14th of February, right after work.

We all look for a perfect card—which, by the way, was already taken. That card is already in the possession of one of the three guys in America who purchased a card well before the Hallmark-infused holiday.

Add to that a good dose of shameful price gouging that arrives with several shakes of cheap red glitter coupled with an insincere message. Of course, it can be recycled year after year on subsequent cases of cards that cost $9.95 each.

Slipping a cellophane sleeve over the front of the card—to battle glitter loss—adds another three bucks to an otherwise horrible poem.

Then we watch.

We watch her open her card. We smile, and we wait. We wait not for the hug, the kiss, the delighted look in her eye; we wait for her to casually glance at the price on the back of the card as she wonders how much she was valued—just like we do when we get ours.

I sent flowers this year. It was far more expensive, and nothing says "I love you" like sixty-nine-dollar flowers that could have been purchased for eleven-ninety-nine just two days ago.

Yes, I added the unnecessary vase—red—so that the flowers can be displayed so that others can believe that I thought about this day far, far in advance.

I guess I did—in fourth grade, Mrs. Hutchinson, halitosis. It all becomes clear to me now.

I just want to let all the guys know that I won't be in the Aisle of Ruin this year. You boys are on your own; I'll miss the camaraderie.

Truth be told, we should probably say the sweet nothings every day and skip the society-mandated, socially acceptable trip to the pharmacy—but only because we should have done it yesterday.

Take your love to lunch, buy them a coffee, give them a call instead of a text. Do something nice. The cards mean nothing if you don't back it up with action.

But don't forget the card, because there is nothing we can do to save you if you do.

VENTI AND HORNSBY

A VENTI-VESSEL OF SILENCE WAS SERVED UP ON THE HOME-stead tonight.

It's as if I walked to the kitchen counter and whispered—to no one in particular—that I would just take the regular.

However, the cacophony of quiet was not the friend I wanted kicking off her shoes and settling in. Not tonight.

I was overwhelmed with a craving for a full frothy mug of something musical. I ordered it with a "little room," and, since I take it black, there was plenty of space for a dollop of piano, a pinch of guitar, and two tablespoons of rhythm.

From across the room, the dump-recovered '80s Klipsch sound-bins served up memories at a medium volume; this is several notches below the levels that a younger man would have wanted his fix delivered.

Since that young man and I parted ways a few years ago, I set the cruise control on a quiet crescendo and leaned back into the mottled-brown accent pillow that defies gravity when I snap awake, lift my head, and focus my eyes on the clock on the far wall while I try to determine if it is time—in fact—to go to bed.

> In your own private place of dreams
> I hope you'll find a place where it seems
> The road is always straight and true
> Wherever you walk is bright for you
> —Bruce Hornsby

Turning off the talking heads and television tirades and re-placing them with the golden vocals of a friend you've never met is my number one suggestion for the new year.

Sleep comes easy when someone sings you a lullaby.

When Good Sardines Go Bad

I perused my food stores the other Sunday. I was apprised that my significant other had recalibrated the cupboards in an earnest effort to protect me from future bouts of food poisoning.

Those were her words, not mine.

She told me about this newfound and—apparently—life-changing event as we drove through the predawn darkness on the way to the airport to send her south to review her own cupboard-keeping habits. I rushed home to survey the work she had done. It's acceptable, but I am missing some perfectly edible staple foods.

She was home for an extended stay, and while she knows I am a planner (not a hoarder), she believes I need to do a better job rotating the crops, or, in this case, the cans.

I tend to stack my canned goods. I buy a bunch, stack them on the shelves, and then I pull from the top. I am reinventing myself and will begin to pull cans and containers from the bottom. This could be disastrous, and noisy, but I am committed to keeping my end of the bargain.

My Campbell's soup stack appears to be untouched, and this gives me hope. I consume it quite often. My collection of tomato soup never sits very long before I need to replace it with fresh stock. I buy it by the flat, and I fall back on toasted cheese sandwiches and tomato soup when I am low on everything else. There is no way that it has a chance to expire.

Thanks to her, I am now low on everything else.

She claims that she found some canned goods that had expired back in 2012. I can't confirm that this is true since she rid our home of the evidence, but I do recall eating some sardines—on crackers—that displayed an expiration date in 2018. They were fine, and I didn't tell her about it. I didn't tell anyone about it (except you). I recall shrugging my shoulders when I popped the top of the tin. I might have mumbled, "Meh," and then dug in.

You can't inform just anyone that you eat sardines, as many folks seem to make the same gruesome gagging vocalization and then ridicule you to no end. If someone sees you eating sardines, they immediately indicate through word and deed that you are stinking up the place. Usually, you are. Eating sardines at work in a well-attended lunchroom is a recipe for being shunned for years.

The way I look at it, someone other than me is eating sardines. When the pandemic-related food shortages hit, I couldn't find a dang can of 'dines anywhere on the shelves. I made it through the drought; I had at least twenty cans in the cupboard.

Can sardines go bad? Ask their mothers, because I have no idea.

The saltines that I utilized during the late-night SOLR (Snacking of Last Resort) were stale, but they were accompanied by sardines. So, there is that. Stale crackers meet the threshold of a delicious side dish when eaten with expired sardines. I don't accept life choices as an either/or situation. I am more of a "things could be worse" kind of guy.

Now, the crackers were not stale because they were aging in place. The saltines were stale because I had run out of clothespins to secure the loose end of the cellophane sleeve that keeps them neatly stacked—and fresh—when tightly sealed.

When I last checked the cupboard, each shelf was full. My judicious inspection caused me to conclude she has halved my kitchen stores. Fortunately, I have more in the basement.

There are beans, soup, Goldfish crackers in the big box, diced tomatoes, tomato paste, spaghetti sauces, Spam, Vienna sausage, and other things. I also have more sardines, and, yup, I have toilet paper, but I don't panic over paper products. I panicked that she might have plucked the pantry of my pre-pandemic Peter Pan peanut butter.

I'd picked up the gigantic tub on one of those days when people were buying everything and anything from the shelves at my local grocer. The mega jar was the last one on the shelf. I grabbed it and have gone through a little over half of it in the past year. The huge jar represented a strange time in America. I believe we have a bond. It still tastes fine, but I am not going to check the date on the jar. In a display of trust toward Peter, I will just keep eating it until it's gone.

Ellie gets her peanut butter for her share of the stale crackers from that jar. We have shared a lot of late-night snacks over the past year. I am having a couple of crackers as I write this missive. Yes, they are a bit punky. They are also perfectly acceptable feeding fodder for my dog and me. We are not high-end.

I am now committed to picking up some new clothespins. Ellie will appreciate more of a crunch with her peanut butter treats, and I'll be completely on my game with fresh crackers the next time I wade into a can of old sardines.

Writing Less, Remembering More

There's been very little writing lately. Storytellers who write stories about not telling stories are—clearly—not going to be nominated for, let alone win, prestigious awards. The only thing I've ever won—to date—is a sixty-inch RCA projection television valued at over twelve hundred dollars. It was on a one-dollar raffle ticket, and I ultimately sold the television to a local pub after a couple of weeks of burning out my retinas.

It was during the mid-'80s, and my grandfather was still alive. He came by one evening for dinner and stayed for an episode of *Matlock*. All Gramps could say was, "His head must be two feet high!"

It was a small living room, and the television had to vie for space with a woodstove and a dog named Jack who felt that the smell of burning fur was an acceptable after-dinner cordial. He would commonly shed the singed hair from his belly because of his love of wood heat.

Ultimately, Gramps got into his Volkswagen van after dinner and motored home. Before he went back into the cold January night, he straightened his bolero tie and told me that I needed a bigger house or to get rid of that ridiculous television. He then pointed out that I needed to put another smoke detector in the hallway.

I couldn't afford that house, let alone a bigger one. I sold the television, put up an extra smoke detector, and Jack continued to sleep too close to the woodstove.

I only write about the television because of a short and memory-inducing conversation with my pal from Ohio. We talk every few weeks. He finally transitioned into an iPhone, so I utilized FaceTime to reach out to him. It was his first experience with the magic of on-camera conversations. Once he took the Scotch tape off the camera so I could see him, we somehow got on the topic of that television. He lived here—in Maine—back in the day.

He said that he pulled into my driveway one night and thought the house was on fire. He claimed that a magnificent glow emanated from all of the downstairs windows.

I had no idea that the television was that memorable, but it was. Paul's vocalized memory sparked the memory of my grandfather's visit for dinner. I think Gramps probably came to that old house about three times in total. Each time he would inspect the chimney connections for the two Vermont Castings stoves. He'd mention that I kept my spare firewood too close to the heat, and he would push the buttons on all the smoke detectors to make sure they were actively protecting us.

Gramps was a twenty-year professional fire chief and a Nazarene minister. We miss him, but I've never once missed that television. I do watch *Matlock* reruns from time to time, and I don't even enjoy the show. With all the new technology and sizes available in televisions, Matlock's head always looks two feet high. Gramps was a visionary, and he knew that there had to be something better than projector televisions.

Memories are what you write about when there are no stories to tell. I hope you don't mind.

You Don't Know What You Don't Know

"You don't know what you don't know." That's one of my favorite phrases.

The first time it crosses your ears, you might think it too simple to add to your list of adages. As you lumber along, you find that it should be your first tattoo.

Sure, Chinese script—touting something terrific—inked up your calf makes you feel dark and ironic. But admitting that you don't know everything makes you more lovable and accepted in groups of other flawed human beings.

I've opted to be a specimen for a group study of the cureless illness that I call idiocy.

Trying to start the snowblower without checking the gas tank first is just one thing I have done, and I've done it on more than one occasion.

I have, several times, found myself wondering if I might have left my coffee mug on the roof of the truck as I drive.

I make amends when I slow down a bit. Then, I focus on avoiding potholes. This suffices as a safety measure until I get to my destination; I'll double-check, then.

You don't know what you don't know.

Recently, while searching far and deep into the Interweb, I've been learning all the ins and outs about slide-in pickup truck campers.

I should note that I doubt my whirlwind trip around the United States will happen, but I'd like to be prepared, just in case it becomes a realistic option.

Today, I learned several ways to sanitarily store soiled sewer hoses. I should tell you that I haven't even pooped in a camper. Yet.

I don't even have a camper. But I am learning storage techniques for hoses that have been tainted by naturally occurring incidents.

Why?

Well, now I know something that I didn't know. I can aptly discuss sewer hose storage techniques with an inquisitive operator of an out-of-state registered Winnebago when they stop to ask me directions, that's why!

I don't need prodding to go one way or another. In the end, I will do—exactly—what I want to do.

If I find my way to travel, it'll be fine once I retire. If—instead—I head to camp and split wood and install some recycled windows so that I can be warmer when the January wind comes off the Atlantic, I'll be just as happy.

I appreciate the cheerleading from those who say, "Just do it." But outside influences have never caused me to do anything that I decided not to do. I've never once felt bad about it. The more fervent someone becomes when driving their opinion down my throat, the more I dig in my heels.

It's one of the reasons that I am disgusted by politicians, pontificators, and humans disguised as journalists. I enjoy finding my way without too much input. Don't even bother telling me the one you like or agree with. I don't care to know.

My sphere of influencers is small, and I'll spend time right there. Maybe I'll set up a camp chair and start a fire.

If you do stop to talk, bring some firewood. Then be quiet. Maybe I am happy not knowing what I don't know. You don't know, and that's the way it's supposed to be.

About the Author

Timothy Cotton retired as a lieutenant from a long career with the Bangor Police Department. He is the author of the best-selling *Got Warrants?* and *The Detective in the Dooryard* and is a recipient of the Erma Bombeck Award for humor. His writing has been published in a number of newspapers, magazines, and websites—most recently CarTalk.com and the *Bangor Daily News*, and the uniform company Blauer also posts a regular podcast narrated by Cotton. He lives in Hampden, Maine.